Compliments
Mrs. Alice Beach Murray

George J Blazier
Jan, 12, 1963

THE CUTLER COLLECTION
of LETTERS *and* DOCUMENTS

1748-1925

LETTERS *and* OTHER MEMORABILIA

of

MANASSEH CUTLER, 1742-1823

EPHRAIM CUTLER, 1767-1853

WILLIAM PARKER CUTLER, 1812-1889

JULIA PERKINS CUTLER, 1814-1904

and

THEIR RELATIVES *and* ASSOCIATES

Gathered and preserved by MRS. MARY DAWES BEACH

Cataloged by MARY LOUISE OTTO, Marietta College

Arranged and Edited by GEORGE J. BLAZIER,
Librarian Emeritus, and Archivist, Marietta College

PUBLISHED BY MARIETTA COLLEGE

1962-1963

RICHARDSON PRINTING CORP.
MARIETTA, OHIO

FOREWORD

The Cutler Family and their descendants have not only made history in the State of Ohio, but recorded it for the benefit of future generations. The Collection of Letters and Documents to be known as the Cutler Collection, is housed in the Dawes Memorial Library of Marietta College, adjacent to the office of the Archivist, where it is classified and safely and securely filed. The card catalogs describe, in brief, the contents of each letter and document. The earliest letter is dated in 1748.

The Collection, numbering more than 5000 items of letters and other memorabilia, was faithfully preserved by the family, beginning with Miss Julia Perkins Cutler, daughter of Ephraim Cutler, her brother, William Parker Cutler, and his daughter, Miss Sarah J. Cutler, and by a great granddaughter of Ephraim Cutler, Mrs. Mary Dawes Beach (Mrs. Arthur G. Beach), to all of whom this volume is dedicated.

GEORGE J. BLAZIER

Archivist, Marietta College

TABLE OF CONTENTS

INTRODUCTION

Ohio history is rich in the annals of its pioneers, who with their sterling characters and industrious habits, their vision for the future, their willingness to brave hardships, migrated from the Western borders of the Colonial states into the frontier. They created an integral part of the United States of America.

Many of those pioneers came from the New England states, where civil life, industry, government and law and order, religious worship, education and culture formed a natural way of life. They had among their numbers farmers, artisans and professional men and women, whose ideals were to establish the culture of New England in the wilderness west of the Alleghany Mountains. They had heard of only a few of the potentialities of the frontier region from the more daring explorers, and of the opportunities for developing the resources in the new land.

Their decisions to migrate to the West were not made overnight, but through a dozen years of hopes dating from the beginnings of the Revolution in 1776 to the culmination of a series of steps that would ensure them laws and government. Their earliest longings had been born in the critical year of 1776, September 20, when the Continental Congress enacted a loosely drawn resolution that the soldiers who would serve until the close of the War should be granted shares in the public lands of the new nation.

After a long period of war, the second step came by a resolution introduced by the representatives of Maryland, that the states of Massachusetts, Connecticut and Virginia cede their Western Colonial grants in the frontier region to the Federal Government for a public domain. The first of the states to surrender its lands was Virginia, in 1784, followed by Massachusetts and Connecticut in 1786.

An important step had been taken in 1781 by the Army officers stationed at Newburgh, New York, while awaiting the outcome of the Treaty of Peace. In a petition, signed by 288 officers, the Congress was asked that bounty lands in the frontier be allotted to soldiers. General Rufus Putnam gave the petition to General Washington, who upon his approval, would present it to Congress.

In 1785, the Congress enacted a land law that would ensure the choosing and owning of lands that would be theirs on the presentation of their Revolutionary land warrants.

A phase of development was proposed by General Rufus Putnam, who recommended to the government that forts be erected in strategic locations along the Ohio River, and farther westward into the frontier. Fort Harmar was established in 1786.

That year is also memorable, that on January 9-10 Generals Rufus Putnam and Benjamin Tupper, the latter reporting on his tour of the frontier, met in Rutland, Massachusetts, to discuss the opportunities for a frontier settlement. This meeting was the origin of the Ohio Company of Associates, a corporation that would purchase a large tract of land west of the Ohio River, and conduct sales from the Federal land offices that would be established. As a result of the night's meeting, the two generals evolved a document, important to both Massachusetts and the future State of Ohio, entitled "A Piece of Information" or as the original record has it "A New Call to Arms," not unlike the sentiments of General Washington to Benjamin Harrison some months earlier.

This circular was meant for general publication in the newspapers, giving a pleasing description of the Ohio country and inviting all officers and soldiers who served in the late war "to become adventurers" and form an association by the name of the Ohio Company. Those who might be interested were asked to meet at appointed places on February 15 and elect delegates who would represent them at a meeting to be held at the Bunch of Grapes Tavern in Boston on March 1.

Accordingly, on the day appointed, eleven delegates met, representing the Massachusetts counties of Suffolk, Essex, Middlesex, Hampshire, Plymouth, Worcester, Berkshire and Barnstable. It is to be noted that five of the delegates were signers of the Newburgh Petition.

Among the delegates representing the county of Essex, was the Reverend Manasseh Cutler, who, in the years ahead, would become one of the leaders with great influence, not only in the outgrowth of the meeting, The Ohio Company of Associates, but in the enactment by the Congress of the Northwest Ordinance of 1787.

The final phase in the series of steps for those who would leave their homes in New England, came on July 13, 1787 which ensured a government comparable to that of the states from which they would migrate. The settlement at the mouth of the Muskingum River and opposite Fort Harmar was the capstone of hopes born in the early Revolutionary years.

Manasseh Cutler, throughout the remainder of his long life, ending in 1823, continued to wield great influence in the affairs of the Ohio Company, the establishment of the first settlements, and the founding of institutions of religion and education. His work was continued by his son, Ephraim, who migrated to the colony in 1795 and became one of the leading citizens of the Northwest Territory in the first half century of the state of Ohio. Ephraim's son, William Parker Cutler, carried on the ideals of his forebears until late in the nineteenth century. Therefore, the Cutler family and their descendants have been leading influences that have made history for the State of Ohio and the nation during two centuries.

GEORGE J. BLAZIER
Archivist, Marietta College

Manasseh Cutler,

CHAPTER 1

MANASSEH CUTLER

Manasseh Cutler, son of Hezekiah Cutler, 1707-1792, and Mrs. Susanna (Clark) Cutler, was born in Killingly, Connecticut, May 13, 1742. His paternal ancestors had been residents of the colony since about 1635, and those of his mother, since 1646.

Possessed with scholarly ambitions, he directed his studies for entering college, selecting Yale as his goal where he was entered in 1761. His ambition while in Yale was to enter the medical profession, and therefore, while adhering to the classical curriculum, he chose all the scientific subjects that were possible, his main study being botany, which in his later life became his most enjoyable avocation. Graduating from Yale in 1765, and planning for marriage soon thereafter, he was offered a position in an importing and trading firm in Edgartown, Massachusetts, which he accepted. After a brief business career, he decided to study along theological lines, placing himself under the tutelage of the Reverend Thomas Balch. On September 11, 1771, he was ordained as a minister, and soon thereafter was called to the pastorate of the Ipswich (later in 1793, renamed Hamilton, Massachusetts) church where he spent the remainder of his professional life.

During the War of the Revolution, he served as a chaplain, successively in three regiments, first under Colonel Francis in the defense of Boston, second, in the brigade of General Titcomb, and finally in the army of General John Sullivan on a raid into Rhode Island.

Interspersed in his early years in Ipswich, he founded and conducted a private school, and also, in order to supplement his meager salary as a minister, continued his medical studies.

Being a leader of influence in his community, he was sought for leadership in public affairs. He was chosen as a director of the Ohio Company of Associates, and in 1800 was elected as a representative to the United States Congress, serving with distinction from 1801 to

1805. He received many honors, among them a doctorate degree from Yale in 1789, and for his scientific researches, was elected to the American Academy of Arts and Sciences in the early years of the Society.

The family of Manasseh Cutler is as follows:
Manasseh Cutler married September 7, 1766 to Mary Balch

Children:
Ephraim Cutler, 1767-1853
Major Jervis Cutler, 1768-1846
Mary Cutler, 1771-1836—Married Joseph Torrey
Charles Cutler, 1773-1805
Lavinia Cutler, 1775-1823—Married Jacob Berry
Temple Cutler, (1), 1778-1778
Elizabeth Cutler, 1779-1854—Married Fitch Poole
Maj. Temple Cutler, (2), 1782-1857

Checklist of Letters and Documents

Manasseh Cutler
Charles Cutler, son of Manasseh
The Ohio Company
The Torrey-Poole Letters
Miscellaneous Letters, 1748
Anderson, Charles
Balch, Benjamin
Balch, Mary (Mrs. Manasseh Cutler)
Bartlett, William
Barton, William
Bentley, _____
Brown, Capt.
Brown, Sophia
Chandler, John J.
Chase, Judge
Cheever, Joshua
Chickering, Mrs. Hannah
Cleaveland, John
Cutler, Charles, son of Manasseh
Cutler, Elizabeth (Mrs. Fitch Poole)
Cutler, Ephraim
Cutler, James P.
Cutler, Maj. Jervis
Cutler, Julia P.
Cutler, Manasseh
Cutler, Mrs. Manasseh (Mary Balch)

Cutler, Mary, (Mrs. Joseph Torrey)
Cutler, Temple, I
Cutler, Maj. Temple, II
Cutler, William P.
Derby, Richard
Dodge, Frank W.
Edmunds, _____
Emerson, Caleb
Everett, Moses
Foster, _____
Friend, Mrs.
Frisbe, Mrs.
Giles, William B.
Glover, John
Greene, Griffin
Herrick, _____
Hildreth, Samuel P.
Kellerman, Prof. W. A.
Lee, Mehitabel Cutler
Merry, Mrs. Elizabeth
Mifflin, Thomas
Moylan, Stephen
Murray, C.
Ohio Company
Ohio, State of
Oliver, Andrew

Oliver, Robert
Parish, E.
Parsons, Theophilus
Pearce, D., Jr.
Pickering, Timothy
Poole, Fitch
Poole, Mrs. Fitch (Elizabeth Cutler)
Poole, William F.
Porter, Ebenezer
Porter, Nathaniel
Putnam, Rufus
Rafinesque, C. S.

Randolph, John
Roche, John
Saltonstall, Leverett
Sargent, Winthrop
Shackleford, Seth R.
Stone, Edwin M.
Torrey, Charles C.
Torrey, Mrs. Joseph (Mary Cutler)
VanInburgh, Capt.
Vourne, V.
Whitney, Elisha

CHAPTER 2

CHARLES CUTLER, SON OF MANASSEH CUTLER

Charles Cutler, third son of Manasseh and Mary (Balch) Cutler, was born at Ipswich, Massachusetts, March 26, 1773. He died at the age of 32 at the home of his brother, Ephraim Cutler at Ames, Sept. 17, 1805.

The Cutler Collection contains only four letters and the cover page of his journal. His correspondents were J. Kidder of New Orleans and Asa Bullard of Boston. See: Catalog of the Cutler Collection in the Dawes Memorial Library of Marietta College.

Letters: Bullard, Asa
        Kidder, J.

CHAPTER 3

THE TORREY-POOLE LETTERS

The two daughters of Manasseh and Mary (Balch) Cutler were married as follows:

Elizabeth to Fitch Poole of Salem, Massachusetts

Mary to Joseph Torrey, also of Salem

Both daughters, their families and descendants, were heirs of their father, Manasseh Cutler, and were bequeathed lands situated in the Ohio Company Tract, administered by Ephraim Cutler, and at his death in 1853, by his son, William P. Cutler.

The Cutler Collection in the Dawes Memorial Library of Marietta College contains 64 letters and documents dating from the early 1800's to 1868.

The following is the index of names and correspondents:

CHAPTER 4

THE OHIO COMPANY OF ASSOCIATES

Professor Archer Butler Hulbert in his monumental work, The Records of the Ohio Company, reviewed the history of the organization and the impact it had on the infant nation which became the United States of America. He wrote in his introduction that "It played an important part in the history of the times; it influenced opinion in the East with reference to western migration; it figured as a factor of no small amount in legislative councils, influenced national legislation with respect to the West, made a dignified and lasting settlement in the State of Ohio where the character of its associates, the honesty of their intentions, and the faithfulness of their performances, for generations, made a vital impress."

The Cutler Collection of Letters and Documents contains several score of the letters of the Directors of the Ohio Company and their associates of the early years of the Company's history fully cataloged in the Dawes Memorial Library of Marietta College. The names of the writers of the letters and their recipients are appended hereto.

Balch, Benjamin
Barton, William
Batchelder, Josiah
Bent, Nahum
Brown, John
Burnham, John
Clap, Daniel
Coburn, Asa
Converse, Alpheus
Cutler, Maj. Charles
Cutler, Ephraim
Cutler, Maj. Jervis
Cutler, Manasseh
Dayton, Jonathan
Devol, Gilbert
Dexter, Timothy
Flint, Royal
Foster, Theodore

Greene, Griffin
Harris, Edward
Harris, John
Isham, Joshua
Ludlow, Israel
Miles, John
Murray, C.
Ohio Company
Oliver, Andrew
Oliver, Robert
Olney, Col.
Parsons, Samuel Holdren
Peters, W. E.
Pickering, Timothy
Platt, Richard
Poole, Fitch
Porter, Ebenezer
Porter, Nathaniel

CHAPTER 5

MISCELLANEOUS LETTERS AND DOCUMENTS,

1748-1923

The Cutler Collection of Letters and Documents contains a group of some three hundred and fifty letters and documents which do not admit of ready classification into the categories illustrating the wide variety of pursuits in which the Cutler Family and their descendants and correspondents were interested throughout the period of more than 150 years from the early life of Manasseh Cutler, 1748, to the last of the descendants living in Washington County, Ohio. Some of the letters are official documents, many others personal from their friends and associates.

The Collection and the large number of classified letters are to be found in the Archives of the Dawes Memorial Library of Marietta College where they are made easily accessible by the catalog of their subjects and names of the writers and recipients. The names are to be found in the following pages of Chapter 5, and in the General Index at the end of this volume.

Barber, David
Barber, Levi
Barker, Col. Joseph
Barker, Joseph, Jr.
Bartlett, William
Barton, Dr. _____
Bates, Edward
Beach, John
Beach, Mrs. Arthur G. (Mary Dawes)
Belknap, Jeremy
Belknap, Miss _____
Belpre
Bennett, Mrs. Margaret
Bent, Nahum
Bingham, Alvan
Bingham, Hiram
Bingham, Luther G.
Bingham, Ralph
Bingham, Silas
Blackburn, _____
Bosworth, D. P.
Bosworth, Mrs. Joanna Shipman
Bosworth, John
Bosworth, John W.
Bosworth, Sala
Bosworth, Sara O.
Brooklyn Eagle
Brown, Mr. _____
Brown & Ives
Brown, Jenny
Brown, Joseph
Brown, Samuel
Brown, William
Browning, William R.
Buck, Aaron
Buell, Joseph
Burnet, Jacob
Burnham, William
Butler, Elijah
Carter, Benjamin
Carville, K. L.
Chandler, Mr. _____
Chappell, Mrs. Amanda B.
Charleston, South Carolina
Chattanooga, Battle of
Cincinnati, City of
Clarke, Robert & Co.
Cole, Philip

Comstock, Elizabeth L.
Cone, Ephraim
Congregational Church
Converse, Wright
Corning, Erastus
Council, John M.
Crothers, Samuel
Cummings, A.
Cunningham, Erastus
Cunningham, John
Cunningham, Martin
Currey, Hiram
Cutler, Ephraim
Cutler, Jervis
Cutler, Manasseh
Cutler, Temple I
Cutler, Maj. Temple II
Cutler, William P.
Dana, Frances White
    (Mrs. Charles Shipman, 1)
Dane, John
Dane, Nathan
Dawes, Ephraim C.
Dawes, Mary,
    (Mrs. Arthur G. Beach)
Dawes, Rufus R.
Dawes, William
Dean, J.
Dean, Silas
Derby, Richard
Devol, W.
Dickerson, Edward
Dix, John
Dodge, Frank W.
Douglas, Stephen A.
Dunlevy, George
Dyar, Charles P.
Edgerton, Luther
Edmunds, Mr. _____
Essex Institute
Evans, Estwich
Farley, Henry W.
Fearing, Paul
Felt, Joseph B.
Ferry Orris
Fisher, Andrew
Fogg, Thomas P.
Foster, Theodore

Fowler, Eliphalet
Francis, Ebenezer
Fraser, Margaret
Friend, Lucy
Fuller, A.
Fullerton, Jarvis
Fullerton, Mr. _____
Gates, Beman
Gates, John
Gilman, Benjamin Ives
Gilman, Joseph
Gilman, Morris
Goss, Daniel
Graham, A. A.
Granville, Ohio
Greenleaf, Samuel
Greene, Griffin
Gregory, Jehiel
Greiner, John
Guthrie, George W.
Guthrie, Stephen H.
Hamer, Thomas L.
Hammond, Charles
Hamson, James
Harpers Weekly
Harris, Rev. Thaddeus
Harvard University
Helb, Jonathan P.
Henderson, Alexander
Hildreth, Samuel P.
Hill, Mr. _____
Hitchcock, Dr. _____
Hitchcock, Enos
Hitchcock, Reuben
Howard, William A.
Huestis, Isaac
Humpheys, Isaac
Humphreys, Joseph B.
Hunt, C. E. M.
Huntington, Gov. Samuel
Hutchinson, William
Hyde, William
Illinois, Map
Independence, Declaration of
Jackson, J.
Jansen, Philip
Jewett, Milo P.
Johnson, C.

Kansas Constitution
Kelley, Alfred
Kelley, William D.
King, Rufus
Kirby, James
Knights of the Golden Circle
Laird, John
Lamson, D.
Lane, J. F.
Lane, P.
Latham, Allen
Lavalette, W. A.
Lincoln, Abraham, Assassination of
Linsley, Jeanette
Linsley, Joel H.
London International Exhibition
Lord, Abner
Loring, George B.
Lucas, Hannah
McClanathan, John
McCready, Aneas
McDougal, John
Maberry, John
Maltbie, Benjamin
Marietta Gazette
Marietta & National Plank Road Co.
Mason, Daniel Gregory
Massachusetts Legislature
Masters, Andrew
Meigs County, Ohio
Meigs, Return Jonathan
Miles, Belinda C.
Miles, Joseph B.
Mills, John
Monroe, Josiah
Morris, Calvary
Morse, John
Murray, John
Neill, Alexander
Newberry, Joseph
New York Republican Convention
Noble, H. W.
North American Review
Nye, Arius
Nye, H.
Nye, Col. Ichabod
Ohio Militia
Ohio Railroad Map

Ohio Soldiers Relief Society
Ohio, State of, Agriculture
Otis, Broaders & Co.
Parker, Mr. & Mrs. _____
Parker, Mrs. Mary
Parker, William
Patterson, J. B.
Patterson, John
Pattin, Thomas
Pearce, David
Pennsylvania Railroad
Perkins, Levi
Peters, Eleazer D.
Philadelphia Sabbath Association
Pierce, T. L.
Plumer, Jonathan
Point Harmar
Pope, H. C.
Post, T.
Powell, E. A.
Powell, O. S.
Prentiss, J.
Price, Frances Dana
Prince, Josiah
Putnam, Benjamin P.
Putnam, David
Putnam, George Haven
Putnam, Mrs. Lucy
Putnam, Rufus
Putnam, William R.
Ramson, W. Z.
Ratcliffe, Richard
Rathbun, Gideon
Rawson, David
Reading, Charles F.
Reily, John
Reynolds, Samuel
Richardson, _____
Ruggles, Benjamin
Safford, Robert
Sanderson, Robert
Satterwaite, E. F.
Sawyer, Artemas,
Scott, William
Sedgwick, Charles B.
Shipman, Charles
Shipman, Mrs. Charles, 1,
    (Frances White Dana)

Shipman, Samuel
Shirley, James W.
Skinner, William
Slavery
Smith, George Plumer
Smith, Joseph
Smith, Polly
Soyez, L.
Spaulding, Elbridge Gerry
Spencer, J. A.
Spofford, Ainsworth R.
Sproat, Earl
Sproat, Ebenezer
Staats, Benoni
Stenson, James
Stenson, Martha
Steubenville Female Seminary
Steward, F.
Stewart, Robert
Stillwell, Samuel M.
Stone, Augustus
Stone, Benjamin Franklin
Stone, Edwin M.
Stone, John B.
Sullivan, Charles
Timby, Theodore R.
True, Jabez
Tupper, Edward W.
Tuttle, Samuel
U. S. Congress
U. S. Sanitary Commission
Vallandigham, Clement L.
Vance, Joseph
VanHorne, Abraham D.
Varnum, James M.
Vaun, William
Wade, Benjamin F.
Walker, E.
Walker, Robert
Walker, William
Walker, William R.
Wallace, Benjamin
Ward, Henry D.
Ward, Nahum
Warner, Philemon
Warren, J.
Warren Township
Washington, George

Eng ᵈ by A.H. Ritchie.

JUDGE EPHRAIM CUTLER.

OHIO VALLEY HISTORICAL SERIES.

Robert Clarke & Cᵒ Publishers, Cincinnati, O.

CHAPTER 6

EPHRAIM CUTLER

Ephraim Cutler, the eldest son of the Reverend Manasseh and Mrs. Mary (Balch) Cutler, was born at Edgartown, Massachusetts, December 13, 1767, and died at Constitution, Warren Township, Washington County, Ohio, July 8, 1853.

At the age of three years he was taken to Killingly, Connecticut, by mutual agreement between his parents and his grandfather, Hezekiah Cutler, and grandmother, Mrs. Susanna (Clark) Cutler, to make his home. He grew up and lived there until he migrated to the Northwest Territory in 1795. The mutual agreement was born out of the fact that his uncle, Ephraim Cutler, brother of his father, had lost his life, May 17, 1766, by a fall from a horse. So great was the grief of his grandparents over the loss of their son they felt that the presence of the young lad in their home would partially assuage their grief and be a comfort to them. This arrangement also gave him the opportunity of acquiring an education under the tutelage of his grandmother where he was taught to read and write and acquire other rudiments of an education. However, he had the advantage of his grandmother's influence but a few years, as her death occurred in 1774. In his later years he wrote "She was an excellent woman, strict in her government, but always kind. I could read well before her death, and had acquired a love of reading which has been a great source of comfort to me, and a lasting benefit."

Upon the death of his grandmother, he was drawn more closely to his grandfather, giving him much assistance, as he grew older, in the operation of the farm and a small mercantile business in Killingly, Connecticut.

Through Ephraim's boyhood years it was always the purpose of his grandfather to provide for him a college education at his father's Alma Mater, Yale College, but the Revolutionary War intervened. But despite the loss of the opportunity for a formal education, he was known throughout his life as a learned man.

About the year of 1775-1776, his grandfather married Mrs. Abigail Robbins. Ephraim continued to assist in running the farm and the mercantile business in the years that his grandfather was frequently called for war service. Upon the deaths of his grandparents in 1791-1792, he became their sole heir. In 1787 he had married Miss Leah Atwood, and like so many other New Englanders at the close of the War, had directed his hopes for migrating to the Ohio country, under the auspices of the Ohio Company in which he owned three shares. He began to plan by closing out the business affairs. The illness of his wife through those years had been such that he felt it necessary to go to the milder climate of the Ohio Company settlement. On June 15, 1795 he and his wife and six children left for the mouth of the Muskingum as he recorded in his memoirs, "hazardous journey and perilous enterprise." With them went Col. Israel Putnam and his family whose destination was the settlement at Belpre. The journey proved to be 'hazardous and perilous,' fraught with delays because of sickness and accidents, and even deaths.

When the party finally reached Williamsport on the Monongahela in Pennsylvania there was a delay of some days until a "Kenticky" flatboat could be completed for the river journey to their destination. In their journey down the Ohio River, they were saddened by the deaths of two of the Cutler children, Mary, the eldest, aged seven years, and Hezekiah, aged one and one-half years, whose unmarked graves were left beside the river near Wellsburg and Wheeling. The family reached the mouth of the Muskingum on September 8, 1795.

Marietta was not the end of the journey for this travel-worn and grief-stricken family. For several weeks Ephraim lay ill in the blockhouse at Campus Martius. As he was slowly recovering, word of their arrival in Marietta reached the Waterford settlement of several families who also had come from Killingly. One of the men, Daniel Davis, came to see Ephraim, and invited him to come to Waterford and share his spacious cabin known as 'the best log house in the country.' Transportation was arranged, canoes and boats for moving, along with clothing and supplies for the winter. Within the year the family moved to a vacant cabin and soon purchased two parcels of land, one tract of four acres, and the other of 68 acres. In his cabin, Ephraim set up a store for mercantile dealings.

Cutler received three commissions to enter the public service, two from Governor St. Clair to be a justice of the peace, and an appointment to a captaincy in the militia. The third commission was from General Rufus Putnam, the Surveyor General, to survey lands. While on his surveys, he heard from peaceful Indians of the presence of a scarce and expensive commodity, salt, in some springs about 40 miles to the north. He with one of his friends, Lt. George Ewing, began developing a business and to form a company for marketing the product.

In 1797, Cutler, Lt. Ewing and Capt. Benjamin Brown arranged for the purchase of larger tracts of land in the area, some 30 miles to the west of Waterford in what was then known as Middletown (Athens) and began moving there, settling on Federal Creek. They were the founders of Amestown, now Amesville, to which place the transportation of household goods and livestock was completed in 1799. The livestock was driven over-land, while the household goods were carried by boats down the Muskingum River, into the Ohio, down to the mouth of the Hocking River, and finally into Federal Creek to the settlement, a distance of 80 miles.

For the next few years, Mr. Cutler devoted himself to the interests of the Ohio Company. Early in this period, he was appointed as an associate judge of Washington County, and in 1801, he was elected to represent the County in the Territorial Legislature. He was also elected as a delegate to represent Washington County at Chillicothe, the Territorial capital, for framing of the constitution for the proposed State of Ohio. As a farmer, he was also engaged in the raising of livestock and droving them eastward over the mountains.

In 1806, he was confronted by his domestic affairs, the lack of a doctor for Mrs. Cutler in the Amestown area, and moved his family to Warren Township, Washington County, where she could have the services of Belpre and Marietta physicians. She died on November 3, 1807.

On arrival in Warren Township, Cutler began planning a home which became known as the 'Old Stone House,' and where he was to spend the remainder of his life. The Old Stone House was an outstanding landmark for Ohio River transportation, and travelers on what was then known as the Lancaster Road, until the early 1870's when the house was destroyed.

> Married, 1787, to Leah Atwood, (1768-1807)
> Children:
>> Mary, 1788-1795
>> Nancy, 1790-1882 (Mrs. Rufus G. Carter)
>> Charles, 1792-1849
>> Hezekiah, 1794-1795
>> Mary (2), 1796-1872 (Mrs. Gulliver Dean)
>> Daniel Converse, 1799-1887

> Married, 1808, to Sally Parker, (1777-1846)
> Children:
>> Sarah, 1809-1896 (Mrs. Henry Dawes)
>> Manasseh, 1810-1822
>> William Parker, 1812-1889
>> Julia, 1814-1904
>> Clarissa, 1816-1874

* * * * * *

Checklist of Letters and Documents

Letters by and to Ephraim Cutler
Charles Cutler, son of Ephraim
Legislature of the Northwest Territory
Constitutional Convention for the State of Ohio
The Ohio Legislature, 1819-1825
Canals and Public Roads
Public Schools
Stock Droving to the East
The Warren Presbyterian Church
The Western Library Association
Trustee of Ohio University

Slavery and the Underground Railroad
The Baltimore & Ohio Railroad
Postmaster at Constitution, Ohio
Newspaper Clippings and Fragments
Historical Articles
Letters to and from his Wife, Sally Parker Cutler
Note and Account Books, Deeds and other Documents
Death and Will
Aborn, Samuel
Adams, Asher

Adams, Lucy
Adams, Paul
Allegheny County, Pennsylvania
Allen, Mary S.
American Home Missionary Society
American Tract Society
Angel, Nathan
Athens, County of
Athens Presbytery
Atkins, Elisha
Atwater, Caleb
Atwood, Leah, Mrs. Ephraim
   Cutler, 1,
Backus, E.
Backus, Matthew
Backus, Thomas
Bacon, John
Bacon, Josiah
Bailey, C. P.
Barber, David
Barber, Levi
Barker, James N.
Barker, Joseph
Barker, Joseph, Jr.
Barkley, Samuel
Bartlett, Henry
Bascom, Ellery
Beaver, John F.
Beelen, Anthony
Beidelman, George
Bennett, John
Bent, A.
Bevier, John F.
Bingham, Alvan
Bingham, Silas
Blanchard, Augustus
Blanchard, Francis
Boothby, Abigail
Boothby, James
Bosely, David
Boyd, Joseph B.
Brainard, Mr. —————
Brasee, John T.
Brawley, Henry
Brewster, Levi
Brooks, John W.
Brown, Archibald G.

Brown, Eli
Brown, Ethan Allen
Brown, John
Brown, Robert
Brown, Samuel B.
Browning, William R.
Buck, Charles
Buell, Timothy
Burnet, Jacob
Burnham, John
Burnham, Thomas
Campbell, Alexander
Carter, Nancy
Carter, Rufus
Cary, Samuel F.
Cass, Lewis
Chambers, David
Chandler, John, Jr.
Chase, Judge
Chester & Barnes
Cist, Lewis J.
Clay, Henry
Cleveland, William
Codding, John
Cole, Philip
Condy, Henry A.
Cone, George
Cone, Timothy
Connell, A. W.
Convers, Charles C.
Converse, Alpheus
Converse, Daniel
Converse, James
Cooley, —————
Corey, John
Corner, Edwin
Cory, Ebenezer
Cowen, Benjamin S.
Crouse, David
Cubage, —————
Curtis, Walter
Cutler, Augusta M.
Cutler, Charles
Cutler, Mrs. Charles, Maria Walker
Cutler, Ephraim
Cutler, Mrs. Ephraim,
   Leah Atwood, 1,

Cutler, Mrs. Ephraim, (2)
(Sally Parker)
Cutler, Maj. James
Cutler, James P.
Cutler, Jervis
Cutler, Manasseh
Cutler, Pliny
Cutler, Temple II
Cutler, William P.
Cutler & Fuller
Dana, George
Dana, Joseph
Danley, William
Dean, Francis
Dean, Capt. Silas
Deane, Samuel H.
Delano, Amasa
Deterly, M.
Devol, Gilbert
Devol, Jonathan
Dexter, Timothy
Dix, John
Dodge, Frank W.
Donalson, Israel
Drake, Samuel G.
Duc, —————————
Dunfee, Calvin
Dunlevy, George
Emerson, Caleb
Este, David K.
Everett, Moses, Jr.
Everett, Moses, Sr.
Everts, Sylvanus
Ewing, Thomas
Fearing, Henry
Fearing, Paul
Fenno, —————————
Friend, John
Fuller, Daniel
Fuller, Philo Case
Gilman, Benjamin Ives
Gitteau, Judson
Good Intent Mail Fast Line
Graves, Isachar
Green, William
Greene, Griffin
Greene, Willard

Gregory, Jehiel
Greiner, John
Grimes, Alexander
Grindstones
Grosvenor, Robert
Halliday, Samuel
Hanks, Rev. Festus
Harper, Daniel
Harris, John
Harvey, James
Haskell, Maj. Jonathan
Hastie, James
Hatch, Elijah
Hawkins, Uriah
Heard, John
Hedges, Josiah
Henderson, Mrs. Hannah
Henry, John
Herrick, Israel
Hibbard, —————————
Hildreth, Samuel P.
Hill, Eli F.
Hobbs, Alfred
House, George
Howard, Horton
Hoyt, Nathan
Humphrey, Charles
Humphrey, Isaac
Humphries, Isaac
Irwin, Hugh
Jackson, Gen. Andrew
Jackson, Henry
Jennings, David
Johnson, P. B.
Johnston, Archibald
Johnston, John
Joline, A. V. D.
Judson, William
Kelley, Alfred
Kennedy, John
Keys, Peyton R.
Kip, John D. W.
Knight, Isaac
Laflin, James
Leavens, Andrew
Leavens, John
Leaving, Joseph

Leigh, Robert
Linzee, Robert
Little, Henry
Loomis, Jacob
Lord, Joseph
Loring, D.
McClanathan, John
McClure, Andrew
McClure, Henry
McDougall, —————————
McFarland, Moses
McGuffey, William H.
McMaster, Gilbert
Marble, Enoch
Mathews, Phineas
Meigs, Return J., Jr.
Menager, C. R.
Middletown (Athens)
Moor, Reuben
Moore, James
Morris, Calvary
Morrow, Jeremiah
Moulton, Joseph
Munro, Joseph F.
Musselman, Henry
Naylor, William
Neale, Thomas
New England Historic
  Genealogical Register
Newhall, Mr. —————————
North American Review
Northwest Territory
Nye, Arius
Ohio Company Lands
Ohio State Life Insurance Co.
Ohio, State of, General Assembly
Ohio University
Olney, Stephen
Olney, William
Parker, Daniel
Parker, David
Parker, Jacob
Parker, Sally (Mrs. Ephraim
  Cutler, 2)
Parker, Silas
Parker, William
Parsons, Enoch T.

Pearce, David
Pearse, Samuel
Pearse, Stephen
Peele, William
Phillips, Isaac
Pierce, J.
Pollock, John B.
Porter, Rev. —————————
Prentiss, Royal
Prentiss, Thomas G.
Putnam, Benjamin P.
Putnam, David
Putnam, Rufus
Putnam, William R.
Rantoul, Robert
Reily, John
Reppert, George
Reynolds, Enoch
Reynolds, John
Reynolds, John R.
Reynolds, Joseph
Riley, James
Roberts, Bennett
Robinson, S.
Ross County, Ohio
Russell, John
Russell, Jonathan
Rutland, Ohio
Safford, Robert
St. Clair, Arthur
Salt, Manufacture of
Saltonstall, Leverett
Sargent, Mary
Sargent, Winthrop
Sawyer, Artemas
Shackleford, Seth R.
Silliman, Wyllys
Skinner, William
Skinner & Barber
Smith, John
Smith, John A.
Sparks, Jared
Spaulding, Rev. —————————
Spaulding, I.
Sproat, Earl
Staats, Elijah
Steamboat, Circassian

Sterrett, William
Stone & Co.
Stone, Augustus
Stone, Benjamin F.
Stone, Edwin M.
Stone, Nathaniel
Stone, Sardine
Storer, Bellamy
Story, Daniel
Strong, Jared
Swasey, Joseph
Swisher, Philip
Texas, Annexation
Tiffin, Gov. Edward
Titcomb, Enoch
Torrey, Joseph
Tredwell, John
Trimble, Gov. Allen
Tupper, Edward
Turner, George
Turnpike, Virginia
Tuttle, Sarah
Tyler, Dean
Vinton, Samuel F.
Wadsworth, Benjamin
Walker, Maria (Mrs. Charles Cutler)
Walker, W. R.
War of 1812
Ward, Henry Dana
Ward, Nahum
Ward, Sarah C.
Ware, ——————
Warren, Dr. John C.
Warren Presbyterian Church

Warren Township School
Washington County, Ohio
Waterman, Mary Ann
Webster, Daniel
Webster, Rev. S.
Webster, Samuel H.
Whipple, Abraham
Whipple, Jesse
White, Haffield
White, Pelatiah
White, Thomas W.
Whitney, Mrs. Elisha
Whitney, James
Whittlesey, William A.
Whittlesey & Harte
Wightman, J. V.
Wilkins, Mr. ——————
Wilkins, Timothy
Wilson, Amos
Wilson, George
Wilson, Joseph
Wilson, Noah L.
Wilson, Newell
Withers, William L.
Wolves
Wood, Ansel
Woodbridge, Dudley
Woodbridge, George M.
Worthington, James T.
Worthington, Thomas
Wright, Gardner
Wyandot Indians
Young, Andrew

CHAPTER 7

CHARLES CUTLER, SON OF EPHRAIM CUTLER

Charles Cutler, the eldest son of Ephraim and Leah (Atwood) Cutler was born at Killingly, Connecticut, on March 30, 1792, and was brought by his family to the mouth of the Muskingum River in 1795. As he grew up, he became accustomed to the forests surrounding his homes, first at Waterford and later in the Ames settlement and soon became an expert in woodcraft, and game hunting with his hounds in the dense woodlands of the Federal Creek Valley.

He received his early education, first at Ames and later away from home at the Muskingum Academy in Marietta. In a letter from his father, dated April 25, 1806, it was noted, "I see that you have improved in penmanship — I hope you will write often."

At the age of fifteen years, he moved with his family to Warren Township on the Ohio River where he grew to manhood, learning the vocation of land surveying.

While a young man, he joined the Ohio militia, serving in the War of 1812 where he was raised to the rank of Colonel. In 1819 he was married to one of his Ames friends, Maria Walker, the daughter of Hon. George Walker, settling on a portion of the lands owned by his father. Later in his life he moved to the village of Chauncey and entered the mercantile business.

In 1849, he went to search the frontiers of the nation as a member of a company bound for the gold fields of California. In a letter written by one of his associates, dated May 17, 1849, while the company was encamped six miles west of St. Joseph, Missouri, the hardships of the trip were described—disease ridden conditions which they had experienced on the route. One week later, May 24, another letter was written from the camp, stating that Charles had died of the dreadful malady of Cholera. He was 57 years of age.

The Cutler Collection of Letters and Documents, now cataloged and housed in the Dawes Memorial Library of Marietta College, contain eight letters written by Charles Cutler and his correspondents:

Carter, Rufus G.
Carter, Mrs. Rufus G. (Nancy Cutler)
Clark, Henry
Cutler, Augusta M.
Cutler, Charles
Cutler, Mrs. Charles (Maria Walker)
Cutler, Ephraim
Cutler, Mary (Mrs. Gulliver Dean)

Cutler, Nancy (Mrs. Rufus G. Carter)
Dean, Gulliver
Dean, Mrs. Gulliver (Mary Cutler)
Nye, Arius
Spaulding, Dr. I.
Walker, Maria (Mrs. Charles Cutler)
Waterman, Mary Ann

CHAPTER 8

EPHRAIM CUTLER AND THE LEGISLATURE OF THE NORTHWEST TERRITORY AND THE FIRST CONSTITUTIONAL CONVENTION FOR OHIO

In September, 1801, Ephraim Cutler was elected the delegate from Washington County to the second session of the Legislature of the Northwest Territory which was soon to assemble at the Capital at Chillicothe. The call came for the meeting of the Assembly while he was on a livestock droving trip to Virginia, and on his return home, he found that he had but a few hours for appearing at the roll call of the first session. Mounting his faithful horse, he departed from his home in Ames for Chillicothe, a distance of 60 miles, arriving there barely in time to answer his name.

Soon thereafter, he was again elected to represent Washington County in the Constitutional Convention which was to meet on November 1, 1802. During the session, which ended with the framing of the Constitution, Cutler was influential in two of its articles, the first, pertaining to anti-slavery, and the second, the article on courts, that instead of having one state court at the capital, to have courts brought nearer to the outlying districts where the citizens would have easier access rather than to be required to make long journeys.

The Letters and Documents pertaining to the Territorial Legislature and the First Constitutional Convention are on file in the

Dawes Memorial Library of Marietta College and made easily
accessible by a complete catalog.

The names mentioned in the correspondence are as follows:

Backus, E.

Cleveland, William

Cutler, Ephraim

Cutler, Manasseh

Darlinton, Joseph

Donaldson, Israel

Fearing, Paul

Finley, Justice

Meigs, Return J.

Morrow, Jeremiah

Northwest Territorial Legislature

Ohio, First Constitutional Convention

Prentiss, Royal

Putnam, William R.

Randolph, John

Reily, John

Safford, Robert

St. Clair, Gen. Arthur

Silliman, Wyllys

Tyler, Dean

Woodbridge, Dudley

CHAPTER 9

EPHRAIM CUTLER AND THE OHIO LEGISLATURE,
1819-1825

Ephraim Cutler's political and social philosophy of life was his
adherence to the fundamental laws of the Northwest Territory, the
Ordinance of 1787, and especially Article III of that document which
reads: "Religion, morality and knowledge being necessary to good
government and the happiness of mankind, schools and the means
of education shall forever be encouraged."

The implementation of this Article, enacted by the Congress,
followed on August 29, 1787 at the third meeting of the Ohio Company which contracted with the government for the purchase of
lands "near the confluence of the Muskingum and Ohio rivers, with
the following provisions: One lot of six hundred and forty acres, in
each township, Section 29, for the purposes of religion;—an equal
quantity for the support of schools & two townships, of twenty-three
thousand & forty acres each, for an university to be established as
near the centre of the whole tract, as may be; which lots & townships are given by Congress & appropriated for the above uses forever."

In the years following the settlement in 1788 of the Northwest
Territory and the admission of the State of Ohio in 1803, religious
organizations were established and in 1804 the University, to be

thereafter known as Ohio University, was chartered by the state Legislature, but the implementation for a public common school system lagged far behind. Private schools had been organized for those who were able to support them, but the children of parents who could not provide for private instruction were deprived of common school education. The Ohio Legislature, from its establishment in 1803 had made no provision for the founding of a public school system. Ephraim Cutler was among the group of citizens who believed that the principles laid down in the Northwest Ordinance had not been fulfilled, and therefore he set out to correct what he thought was a violation of the fundamental law, by seeking a seat in the Legislature where his and other voices could be more effective for the establishment of a common school system. In 1819 he was elected to the Legislature on this platform and became a member of the House of Representatives. He was re-elected in 1820. Two years later, 1823, he was elected to the Ohio Senate and re-elected in 1824.

In 1821, a bill for the first school law was passed by the House of Representatives, but was defeated in the Senate. However, Cutler's crusade for a common school system was continued, and, with the help of other likeminded legislators he succeeded to a point where Governor Allen Trimble was authorized to appoint a committee for a study of the situation and make recommendations for placing the matter again before the Legislature. The members of the committee who may be known as the founders of the common school system were Caleb Atwater, Josiah Barber, James Bell, Rev. John Collins, Ephraim Cutler, Nathan Guilford and James Hoge. After three years of study and investigations, the first adequate school bill was brought to the Legislature and passed by both Houses.

It is recorded that when the bill was passed by the House of Representatives Cutler stood by Nathan Guilford, a member of the Committee and said "Lord, now lettest thou thy servant depart in peace, for mine eyes have seen thy salvation."

While in the legislature, Cutler was ever the proponent of bills for public roads, turnpikes and canals, all of which were enacted into laws.

The Cutler Collection of Letters and Documents, including the correspondence of Cutler's legislative years, are a part of the Manuscript Collection in the Dawes Memorial Library of Marietta College.

The names of the correspondents and recipients of the letters are as follows:

Adams, Demos
Adams, John Quincy
Baker, Isaac
Barber, Levi
Barker, Joseph
Barker, Samuel
Bent, A.
Brown, Archibald G.
Brown, Gov. Ethan A.
Brown, John
Brown, John II
Brown, Samuel
Buell, Timothy
Bureau, W. W.
Canals
Cary, Samuel F.
Chambers, David
Clay, Henry
Coffinberry, Andrew
Cogswell, Eli
Conant, Dr.
Connell, A. W.
Converse, Daniel
Cooke, E. Leutherios
Corner, Edwin
Corp, Benjamin
Cowles, R. W.
Culbertson, James
Cutler, Daniel
Cutler, Ephraim
Cutler, Mrs. Ephraim, (2)
    (Sally Parker)
Cutler, Julia P.
Cutler, Sarah (Mrs. Henry Dawes)
Dana, Joseph
Dawes, Mrs. Henry (Sarah Cutler)
Dawes, William M.
Devol, Jonathan
Devol, William
Dodge, Frank W.
Dunbaugh, _____
Emerson, Caleb
Fearing, Paul
Findley, N. C.
Fuller, Timothy

Gates, Beman
Guernsey County
Harrison, Robert
Hebbeth, E.
Hedges, Josiah
Hildreth, Samuel P.
Humphreys, Isaac
Joline, A. V. D.
Kilbourne, James
King, Nehemiah
Knight, James
Laflin, James
Lance, J.
Lane, _____
Laughton, _____
Lindley, Jacob
Lord, Abner
Mathews, John
Ministerial Lands
Morris, Calvary
Morrow, Jeremiah
Nelson, Daniel
Northrup, Col. Henry
Nye, Anselm T.
Nye, Horace
Ohio, Legislature
Olmstead, P. H.
Osborn, Ralph
Osburn, Ezra
Ossoli, Margaret Fuller
Putnam, Edwin
Parker, Jacob
Parker, Sally (Mrs. Ephraim Cutler, 2)
Perkins, Elephaz
Peters, J. A.
Putnam, Aaron W.
Putnam, Benjamin P.
Putnam, David
Putnam, Douglas
Putnam, Israel, III
Putnam, William R.
Regnier, J. B.
Reily, John

CHAPTER 10

EPHRAIM CUTLER AND STOCK DROVING

The Life and Times of Ephraim Cutler, written by his daughter, Julia Perkins Cutler, and published in 1890, contains, besides other facets of the life of the subject, his efforts for enriching the economy of the settlement by encouraging the raising of livestock which he would purchase and drive over the mountains to the Eastern Markets.

In the book, The Life and Times of Ephraim Cutler, pages 89-90, is to be found an excerpt from the Cutler diaries: "When I resided in Ames township, with a view to encourage settlers to come into that part of the country, I bought on credit a considerable amount of land from proprietors in New England, which I sold to settlers on credit, trusting them until they could raise wheat or cattle, usually the latter, to pay me for their farms. This early led me into the droving business. I commenced this traffic in 1800, and it was said that I drove the first cattle over the mountains to eastern markets ever taken from Ohio. I did more or less of this laborious business, annually, for thirty years. Eventually, many poor families were placed in very flourishing circumstances, who had nothing with which to buy land, nor a dollar to spare for years after they made the purchase of me. I thus aided some two hundred families to acquire homes."

The Cutler Collection of Letters and Documents, now housed in the Dawes Memorial Library of Marietta College, includes some fifty letters, written and received by Cutler, together with some most descriptive narratives of his over-the-mountain journeys, to his wife, Mrs. Sally P. Cutler. The list of the names of the writers and recipients is as follows:

Brown, William
Browning, William R.
Cone, Timothy
Cutler, Ephraim
Cutler, Mrs. Ephraim, (2) (Sally Parker)
Dodge, Frank W.
Fearing, Paul
Gardner, James B.
Gilman, Benjamin Ives
Grayson, B. O.
Harper, Daniel
McClanathan, John
Maryland, State, of, Backbone Mountain
Maryland, State of, The Glades
Maryland, State of, Hagerstown
Maryland, State of, Williamsport
Maryland, State of, Yough Glades
Parker, Sally, (Mrs. Ephraim Cutler,) (2)
Putnam, David
Safford, Robert
Scioto River Valley
Stickler, Jacob
Stone & Co.
Stone, Augustus
Vaun, William
Virginia, State of, Loudon County
Virginia, State of, Moorefield
Virginia, State of, Romney
Walker, Archibald, B.
White, John White

CHAPTER 11

EPHRAIM CUTLER AND OHIO UNIVERSITY

Ohio University was originated out of two meetings, first the Ohio Company on August 29, 1787, and second October 27, 1787 when the contract was signed by the Board of Treasury and the Ohio Company, for the purchase by the Ohio Company of 750,000 acres. The contract also reserved two townships, or 46,080 acres of land at the center of the Ohio Company's tract to be used for a university. The name of the institution of learning was designated by Manasseh Cutler as THE AMERICAN WESTERN UNIVERSITY.

The implementing of the clause for the reservation of the lands of the two townships was delayed by the Indian Wars. In 1795, General Rufus Putnam, who had the charge of the university townships urged that immediate steps be taken to make the land productive and "Thus provide a fund to commence an institution." In the meantime some twenty "Squatters" had moved into the lands, hoping to receive titles as soon as the Territorial Legislature convened. The Legislature in its meeting on Dec. 18, 1799, made provision for surveying the lands as the first procedure toward creating the university. General Putnam, after having examined the lands of the two townships, the rentals of which would amount to over $5,000, suggested steps for the erection of buildings and appointment of officers. The next step, enacted by the Territorial Legislature, Jan. 9, 1802, passed an act authorizing the institution.

General Putnam, on May 21, 1802, called a meeting of a number of men who would be trustees, but the establishment was delayed until the new State of Ohio was ordained in 1803. The final act authorizing the founding of the institution came on February 18, 1804, the name to be OHIO UNIVERSITY.

Cutler was elected to the Board of Trustees in 1819 and served for more than thirty years. Throughout his trusteeship he was the ever dependable lobbyist in the Legislature for providing funds. He also advocated the founding of a medical college but financial difficulties proved too great for such a step in that period.

The Cutler Collection of Letters and Documents in the Dawes Memorial Library of Marietta College, includes the correspondence of Ephraim Cutler through this trying period. The names of the correspondents are appended hereto.

Alexander, John
American Western University
Athenian Society
Atwater, Caleb
Barber, Levi
Bartlett, Henry
Bingham, Alvan
Brasee, John T.
Brough, John
Brown, Archibald G.
Brown, J. M.
Cutler, Clarissa
   (Mrs. James S. Walton)
Cutler, Ephraim
Cutler, Manasseh
Cutler, William P.
Dana, Joseph
Gates, Nathaniel
Hay, Henry
Howe, H. R.
Irvine, James
Joline, A. V. D.

Lindley, Jacob
McGill, Dr. _____
McGuffey, William H.
Ohio University
Pratt, E.
Perkins, E.
Putnam, Edwin
Putnam, Rufus
Rice, Theresa
Riley, James
Ryors, Alfred
Tallmadge, Benjamin
Thomson, James
University Townships
Wale, William
Walker, E.
Walton, Mrs. James S.
   (Clarissa Cutler)
Wilson, Pres. Robert G.
Woodbridge, Dudley
Worthington, Gov. Thomas

CHAPTER 12

EPHRAIM CUTLER AND THE BALTIMORE
& OHIO RAILROAD

The Baltimore & Ohio Railroad, chartered in Baltimore early in 1827, to be built in a westerly direction, created great hopes in Marietta for a mechanical transportation outlet for marketing of agricultural and manufactured products of the rapidly expanding American West.

Within a few weeks after the Charter became effective, a public meeting was called for April 9, 1827, to take measures to induce the Directors to make Marietta a point for building the Road to the Ohio River, possibly at Williamstown. Resolutions were adopted and a committee of seven composed of Joseph Barker, Jr., President, Nahum Ward, Secretary, Col. Joseph Barker, Dudley Woodbridge, Dr. Samuel P. Hildreth, James M. Booth, William R. Putnam, and John Mills was appointed to carry out the enterprise.

In August of that year, a party of surveyors, under the leadership of Col. Joseph Barker, set out for Clarksburg, Virginia, to explore practical routes over which a railroad might be built.

Construction moved slowly from the eastern terminus at Baltimore and at the end of a decade the Directors had not reached a decision for extending the Railroad into the mountains.

Becoming impatient with the slow progress, the Marietta Committee, on March 13, 1837, commissioned Ephraim Cutler to travel a proposed route from Marietta to Baltimore to arouse interest along the way in building the Road. His commission included remaining in Baltimore as long as possible to promote the plan with the Board of Directors to build their line from Winchester, Virginia, or near there, to Romney, Clarksburg, and "to this place."

Armed with letters of introduction to the President and Directors of the Railroad, including Johns Hopkins, Ephraim Cutler set out within the week, on horseback, on his important mission, and, almost daily he wrote letters back to members of the Railroad Committee, and to his wife, Mrs. Sally Parker Cutler.

His first letter, sent to his wife, reported his sojourn at Clarksburg, Virginia:

April 3 (1837)

My Dear:

I arrived here on Saturday morning and by the goodness of Providence who ever cares for us escaped in passing the Monongahela altho the water was nearly over my horses' back. I received no other damage than having my boots filled & my clothes some wet not my saddle bags.

I presume some person observed me reading my Bible and in consequence, I was taken for a Clergyman and accordingly a respectable gentleman, a Mr. Lewis, called on me yesterday, the Sabbath, and stated that their clergyman was absent and respectfully invited me to supply his place—don't laugh too much.

This day early I was called on by this Mr. Lewis who introduced Dr. Gettings, a son-in-law of Mrs. Jackson, daughter of Mr. Meigs to whom I had a letter & during most of the forenoon my room was crowded with auditors. Dr. Getting invited me to Dine and the afternoon has been taken up with a very respectable meeting of the citizens of the town and county who invited me to give them Information on the subject of my mission. I, of course, made some what of an effort—was heard with riveted attention—the meeting passed several resolutions approbationary of the subject, appointed a committee to memorialize the Balt. & Ohio R. R. Directors, etc. This far so good.

Last night I returned to rest in a chamber where a coal fire was made and about one o'clock I was awakened very nearly stifled with smoke and found the floor ready to burst into flame—the room filled with smoke to a greater degree than I ever before saw. I made out to get the Pitcher of water set to wash and put out the fire & opened the door and was able after some effort to breathe freely.

O how much we are dependent on Him who cares for us. If to return I may have many Incidents to relate which may amuse some of you. I must devote the rest of the sheet to Wm. with feelings of affection I am yours as ever.

EPHRAIM CUTLER

B. & O.

Dear Wm   Apr. 3, 1837

I would call your attention to the case of Sandy Cole's notes, it is possible he came over or you may see him & if so I believe that it is best to tell him if he will make out one third of the money soon, say 1st of June, give his notes for one third to be paid in one quarter & remainder on 29th. I will take it so & will of course stop the suit. You will call on Mr. Emerson for the note, if needed.

If Mr. Kingsbury has occasion to write to me inform him to direct to me to the care of Tiffany, Devall & Co. Baltimore. This will be the way I shall receive letter & direct your letters in the same manner.

My horse performed better than my fears were, thus will walk 33 to 35 miles a day.

Expect to leave early in the morning—the proceedings of the meeting here are to be published in the papers at Clarksburg, Parkersburg, Winchester, Baltimore and Marietta. There was more excitement than I expected.

(Signed) Parent, E. CUTLER
Baltimore, April 17

1837

My Dear Wife:

The first and dearest of my heart. I have now to say that an ever gracious Providence has cared for me, preserved me in every danger, seen and unseen and I arrived here Sunday evening, coming from Winchester, Va., 120 miles on a rail road through on that day travelling about 9 hours.

My journey from Marietta to Winchester was Pleasant in finding many early old Friends recognizing me in finding my mission approved of by the intelligent gentlemen altho a general despondence seemed to have prevailed and in being preserved in some alarming cases of danger but I had two days free from storms of rain or snow—two severe snow storms. Saturday I delivered a letter to Mr. James Thompson with whom I had a Slight acquaintance. He is a very handsome manner—Invited me to take up Quarters with him (a rich old bachelor) to which I consented & yesterday attended with a connection of his (a Mr. McGowen) he being himself Quite unwell, and heard Mr. Dunean, an excellent minister lecturing from the 8th Ch. of Romans. Seldom have heard a more impressive discourse or one entirely satisfactory to me. Mr. Thompson has a Niece to take charge of his house—a fine young lady which is the only white person I have yet seen at Table.

The Proceedings in respect to the railroad had at Clarksburg is being published in all the Balt.—Papers. But the terrible crash in such immense failures at N. Orleans & more especially at N. York have alarmed, convulsed & confounded all—and nothing could be more in opposition to my hopes or success in my Mission. I am, however, not discouraged but have confidence that I shall not labour in vain—but that a gracious providence will turn all to his own honor & Perhaps in my weakness & in the opposing difficulties in the end a result which will consummate in Advancing the interest of our common country & Washington County & Marietta in particular.

You have no doubt heard ere this that Failures to the amount of many millions at N. Orleans fell by about 150 (illegible) in N. Y. &

some a/c say 90 millions—this Appalling State of things places me in trying circumstances. On full and mature reflection I have determined not to relax my endeavor to draw attention to the great object in view. And I am proposing a memoir to lay before the Board of Directors of the Rail Road Company explaining the situation of our section of the country with the future Prospects of usefull & extended improvements from Marietta and different Points on the Muskingum—the task is arduous & requires talents, investigation and a happy manner to place it formidably and plainly before them which I can by no means pretend to—I have come to the conclusion that duty requires this of me & must therefore trusting also in the Gracious Goodness of the Giver of every good and perfect gift for his aid in the performance—

My intense confidence in you and Wm. to be able to overcome any adverse circumstance that may have taken place & the situation in which I am at present placed have made it necessary for me as far as possible to forget about home anxieties—but its inmates are ever present in my mind—one other also ever dear our dear Sarah as well as our dear Polly all for feeling which cannot be divided. I must leave you all in the kind care of Him who has ever cared for us.

I cannot come to any conclusion about anything respecting my future operations further than I have already stated.

I found a letter here (Inclosing to introduce me to Mr. McLane the late secretary of the Treasury) from Mr. Ewing—his recommendation I think would make my children a little proud of their Dear father if they were to see it.

At Winchester I sold Charley Blackey horse. I am concernedly anxious to hear from you all & presume that I shall be shortly gratified.

EPHRAIM CUTLER

Baltimore, April 25, 1837

My ever Dear Wife:

Your ever welcome favor of the 11th rec'd after a suspense painfull in deed you and Julia must for the present be content with heart-memory for the Present.

It is probable you will not write again—I cannot say when I shall be through with this perplexing business—I have found the directors of the Bal. & O. R. R. very ignorant of Ohio of some of the geography of that portion of Country which they ought to have been well acquainted with—A Friend told me that since I came one of the Directors told him that Marietta was 250 miles further from Balt than Wheeling & insisted that it must be at least 150 further a least—however I have not talked with an intelligent man here that after the Whole Matter was explained but what freely acknowledged that the route by Marietta ought to be adopted.

I have letters from Mr. Ewing & Vinton to Hon. Lewis Mc.Lane Prest of the R. R. Co of a flattering character but he is in New York & of course I shall not see him—I have found here a Mr. James Thompson who once lived on Hocking with whom I had formerly had a slight acquaintance—

I have not yet seen the board together & am not certain that I shall untill May 3. I have proposed a Memorial & got it printed (sent him one) which I expect to present to them—

It has cost me time and much reflection to prepare it, such as it is, it must go. I have had every attention paid me yes more, much more than I deserve—

You have probably seen that the Clarksburg People have been Praising my address to them but I have tried but I must rely alone on Him who is able to support me—never was there nor can I conceive it possible there can be a **** time to make a useful impression—the duty therefore is severe.

I hope I shall be sustained—if I am appointed a Com n to the G.A. (General Assembly) & get the appoint by a letter from Mr. Kingsbury. I believe I shall attend at Phila but do not think I shall go farther than that East.—Believe if I had closed my business hear & had rec d his letter I should start for N. E. to morrow—remember at the throne of Grace.

With the utmost affection, I am as ever

Your ever loving husband

Ephraim Cutler

"I should start home as soon as I had done with the R. R. Company had I not given encouragement that I would attend the Gen¹ Assembly—I have scarcely settled what I shall do yet.

I am indeed homesick—but have met with the kindest & most respectful treatment.

Clarissa's excellent letter came yesterday, Post Mark-d 21st double postage, write single on your letters when they are so

Oh how I want to see you a; ! Give my love to all the Family and remember me without (being) at the throne of Infinite Mercy.

I am your affectionate Parent

Ephraim Cutler

April 27, 1837

Dear William:

The danger of taking bank paper that is worth nothing is now great. The consternation respecting Failures of large brokerage establishments and banks I believe is well founded. I have little doubt it will extend much further than what it is at present—it is probable that no portion of our Country can escape disastrous consequences. Be careful not to take, on no account, of Bank paper from any distant banks. I would confine the exception to Marietta, Lancaster, the Franklin bank of Columbus & Chillicothe & no others. I do not know that you will be in the receipt of any other on hand and have a call to pay out save the above named in preference of all others. If you can see Charles or let him know what I have written above be sure to do it.

I fear our Stone making will have a considerable amount on our hands of Dead property. ——————— Times are fearfully bad & the most Intelligent men here look for worse. Don't have any more help.

I have not yet presented my Memorial to the Board of the R. R. Company—shall probably know in a few hours when and where I can do it. There is no forcing anything along. I feel very unhappy but must bear it—I find a much more favorable opinion respecting the object of my Mission since I circulated a few copies than before. It has been declared here as an important and valuable document.

EPHRAIM CUTLER

New York, May 1st, 1837

My dear wife and Children:

I left Balt.—1 on Sunday 28th came first day to Phil-a—arrived about 2 P.M. arrived here about the same hour Saturday. Yesterday I visited Sabbath 2, & went to meeting & sat in the pew with the family of that distinguished man. the late Harlan Page. I cannot describe to you my feeling on entering the domicil parlour & beheld the library hanging up by the Wall side.

Oh, how far short do all come of that excellent man—who of us can expect to hear the unspeakable welcome like him—well done thou good and faithful servant—enter into the Joy of thy Lord.

I have had much to be thankful for—at Balt—I was introduced to Dr. Coe of Indianapolis, a very interesting man—I found him on board the S-boat & he has been my companion since he is well acquainted at Phil-a & there was introduced to M-r Louis McLane whose being there was in part the reason of my coming on—he is Pres-t of the Balt. Ohio R. R. & it was thought by my friends to be important to see him.

I had at Bal-t Letters of introduction from Messrs Ewing and Vinton. I have just been introduced to him by Dr. Coe & was rec-d with Politeness and respect to spend the evening with him & on the morrow move forward for Boston & ———————

I have seen H. D. Ward—expect to dine there tomorrow & start at 5 o-clock. All is confusion & Dismay. A Gent-l told me here that he had witnessed the Embargo—the War & the Great Conflagration here but never before witnessed so much dismay and distress as at Present— how it will end is known to Him who rules and governs according to his will and perhaps he will bring order & prosperity out of this Invisible state of things—it will be well with those who amidst these Judgments Learn Righteousness & with the proper spirit submit to his sovereign will & Pleasure—

I wrote to Wm Just before I left Bal-t—I had not then decided to come on here—I believe I decided in 1 hour after I put the letters in the Office—I came early the next morning.

My whole course here has been a trying one I have scarcely

page thirty-three

known what to do—I now sometimes hope that a kind and Gracious providence will favor the Enterprize & and that my labor will not all be in vain. I think at present prospects are, on the whole favorable but of any good results attend it—we ought to attribute it to him who governs in the hearts of man & doth his pleasure & none can resist his will.

I never needed your united prayers more. I am old—infirm—find many things as Proper—have an earnest desire that this Probably last Public act may prove beneficial to my country all makes it important to supplicate—divine mercy on him—I hope I shall place my whole reliance.

Yours in loving bond of affection
EPHRAIM CUTLER

EPHRAIM CUTLER
N. York, May 1, 1837

Gentlemen of the R. R. Committee

I wrote a few hasty lines after my arrival at Bal^t stating as well as I remember that I thought it necessary to prepare a memo to be presented to the Pres^t & Directors of the R. R. Co.

I found it to be important to have this printed to enable me to Place my views & yours more distinctly not only before the 24 (29) Directors but also other influential men, I presume that several of you have, ere this, rec^d a Copy.

I was Introduced to several members of the board to who I explained that men appointed to so important a trust knew so little about what ought to have been the primary Qualification—the Geography of this portion of the Country—a Friend assured me that in conversing with one of these Gen^t Dir that he asserted that Marietta was 250 miles farther from B— than Wheeling & with all of them the importance of Wheeling was duly magnified—I obtained the Publication in all the papers (through our Friend) of your report which excited much attention beleaving also that the opinions of People has undergone some change, and also beleaving that a part of these Hon^l Directors are mear men of _____ easily moulded by a master spirit and having been assured that the President M^r McLane was not only unpledged but fully open to conviction and being urged by our Friends here to see him before I presented the memo formally to the Board. I have come on here for that purpose. I rec^d Letters of Introduction forwarded to Bal^t from the Hon^l messrs Ewing & Vinton & I have had the honor a few minutes ago to present them to M^r McLane—and have Rec^d assurance from him that the subject was left open where the road should reach the Ohio or he otherwise would not have accepted the appointment. In the *short* Interview I have had with him I caught considerable that was Favorable he appointed this evening a further appointment for me—explain your wishes, etc.—You are all aware of the Terrible state of the Monetary business throughout our Country. My situation has been a trying one, perhaps it would have been more satisfactory to have immediately returned without making an effort from an anxious and careful review of the whole ground. I have decided otherwise.

I have a strong desire to go on to Boston. I shall determine that matter after my interview with Mr. McLane but conclude from a word that was dropt from him that he will conclude to be in Baltimore in about three weeks—in which time, if a kind providence should favor me I can meet him and the members of the Board.

I shall indeed be disappointed if I do not succeed in procuring a reexamination & survey of our route—and this is all that can now be expected.

When I got to Baltimore I found that most of the money I brought was little better than blank paper. If I could have a draft of the $50 forwarded to me at Baltimore it would be a relief—direct to the care of James Thompson, Commision merchant at Donnel's wharf or Messrs Tiffany, Devol Company. Mr. Thompson has rendered very essential service.

With feelings of respect I am your devoted servant,

EPHRAIM CUTLER

P.S. 10 o'clock, evening.

I had a most gratifying visit with Mr. McLane—he has taken the memorial & your expo- will send to Baltimore tomorrow and I have agreed to call on him on my return—he assures me that if he remains as President (of which I believe there is little doubt) an examination of our route shall be made and that we shall have sufficient Notice before there is any definite action respecting the Ultimate determination —is said (to enforce our wishes) which he thinks will not take place under a year hence—he will write to have a resolution passed to have the route surveyed which I hope to have the pleasure of being the bearer when I return. I had the pleasure to have the company of H. D. Ward to whom I am under great obligation for assisting me in the explanation I made. Shall leave tomorrow at 5 o'clock for the East— expect to return in about two weeks.

E. CUTLER

Letter of May 1 to the Gentlemen of the R. R. Committee:

I found at Baltimore that 5 parties of Civil engineers, at the expense of the United States are now examining the route, first to Boonsboro & Hagerstown, second to Cumberland & the mouth of the Savage by Winchester & Romney, Virginia. I have a long conversation with Mr. McKnight, the head of the party who did not hestitate to give his opinion —be most adapted to having a lateral road from Romney to Cumberland and that the main stem would go direct to Savage and up that creek, Crabtree, over the Backbone near Armstrong in the Glades. The third party from Backbone to Wheeling, the fourth from Cumberland up Wills Creek by Castleman river & to Pittsburgh, and fifth from Cheat river to Parkersburg—it therefore appeared to me that now is the time, if ever, to procure an examination towards the Muskingum. I have also one thing to encourage me and the Importance to our portion of the country as also in the largest point of view to our beloved country makes it indeed highly important that the nearest, the best route should be fixed on.—I believe I may venture to say that I had convincing proof both while on the way & at Baltimore that many Intelligent and interesting men are not convinced that the route we advocated is the one to be adapted for the country's Greatest benefits & I have been urged to persevere have come on so far now.

E. Cutler

Philadelphia
May 27, 1837

Dear Wm.:

I arrived here on my return yesterday at 12 noon. I have never during my life had in the same length of time so much enjoyment from the time I wrote you at Baltimore, I believe dated on the 27th of April. I had a prosperous journey on East at New York. I had an interview with Louis McLane, President of the Baltimore & Ohio Railroad. He gave me every appearance of his assistance in procuring the survey of the route by C. (Cumberland) to Marietta and appeared convinced that the route ought to be adopted when the Company came to the first conclusion on that subject.

Left New York at 5 P.M., arrived at Killingly next day at 2 P.M. Found my excellent old minister in his 87th year as _____ as in his youth an entirely graceful gentleman in his manners. He said, when I was introduced, my father, Cutler.

Cutler _____ he once knew Ephraim Cutler but he removed a long time ago to the West. "I am the man, said I." He clasped me in his arms and was so agitated that it took him some time to recover himself. At length he said "their is not a man in the world that could be gladder to see." I was received everywhere in the most flattering manner. On Sabbath I had the satisfaction to join in commemorating the dying love of our dear Redeemer with a number of my old friends and with the offspring of numbers now gone to their eternal home.

Col. _____ Torrey devoted his time, horse and chaise in carrying me about so that I had the opportunity of seeing the vast improvements which are astonishingly great in Killingly. It is to me now the Pleasantest place I ever saw except home.

Monday, left at 11, A.M. arrived at Boston, via Worcester 7 A.M., arrived at Salem, 10 A.M. and then Brother Poole, 11 A.M. Called at Dr. Torrey's but he was out. He came up soon after, found Brother Poole sick, also, Leonard. Dr. Torrey, with Brother Poole's horse and chaise took me to Hamilton where I saw Augusta, oldest daughter, Rev. Mr. Kelly, who inquired after you continually. Dr. Torrey's son _____ in Beverly and Temple on my return to Boston which I left on Monday, 1 P.M. by Providence Railroad. Left Providence 4 P.M., encountered a terrible storm in the passage to New York. Arrived there Tuesday, 1 P.M. Wednesday, left New York at 5 A.M., arrived at Philadelphia at 12 noon, and here I am. Went to the General Assembly (Presbyterian) heard sermon by Dr. Witherspoon, text, First Corinthians, 1st chapter, verses 2-11. Dr. Dickinson was chosen Moderator by a vote of 133 to 106. Dr. Dickinson was from Lane Seminary. Discussed Old School (Presbyterian) affairs.

Now for your letters by Mr. Roberts. I am pleased with McClure's joining in the stone business, but fear that there will be no opportunities for selling any this year, occasioned by the overturn in money matters. It is beyond all description. A Mr. Allen who visited me more than 30 years ago in Ohio, a most respectable man in New York said he had seen the Embargo and the conflagration and the war and that all put together did not occasion as much distress as this dreadful disaster, so said one of the first men in Philadelphia. Since I arrived here more than 100 Irish have left New York in the boat with me and are now either here or in the country hunting for something to do. At Lynn, the shoemakers were leaving in great numbers, distress in the extreme is everywhere felt among the laborers, and the rich are becoming poor.

I do not wish to have the wool sold unless you can obtain cash for it, if anyone will give that at 40, sell, but I expect that you cannot get anything for it. I had rather keep it than to trust anyone there I know. No knowing whom to trust nor where these things will end. The Lord reigns and that is different as a nation. We deserve all we are experiencing and much more as individuals we merit not for His forbearance and long suffering much and the blessings we are constantly receiving at His hand. I have been preserved in the most eminent dangers again and again since I left you and what poor return am I making for his kindness over me. Oh, let me not forget the hand that leads and guides us through all our ways.

I think you are quite premature in contracting for building the M. H.

I cannot tell you when the assembly will be likely to adjourn—an evening session is anticipated. I shall return by the kind providence by Baltimore and Pittsburgh and attend to the stone concern.

The balance of the sheet to Ma'am and the girls.

My Dear Family:

You cannot even conceive how much I want to return to your kind embrace. I am too old to be away from home of all places the most proper for such an old and worn-out thing as I am. (He was 70 years old). A gracious Providence has constantly provided for me and I have everywhere found friends in abundance, contrary even to my hopes. I think I have succeeded in my mission. I expect to attain all I asked from the Baltimore & Ohio R. R. Company for at last the President has promised it. The manner that my old friends and neighbors received me overwhelms me. A real excitement seemed to prevail throughout the Killingly neighborhood. All flocked around me and joy seemed to sparkle from every eye. I have a fine specimen of Granite for your cabinet. I cannot bring home much of anything of value.

I wrote to Henry Dawes some description of my reception by Mr. Atchison and requested him to forward it to you.

Before I left Batimore I was discouraged, worn out and homesick —despairing of effecting anything and was requited exceedingly when I went to the fountainhead, Mr. McLane. I found that I could make an impression and he appeared gratified with the memorial I had written and was not backward in giving me encouragement. I asked about the monetary concerns of the country and if they prevent the progress for building the road at present.

But every hour seems like a day and every day a month while here but twill not do to put the hand to the plow and look back.

Tell Mr. Kingsbury that a namesake and relation of his belongs to this body (The Presbyterian Assembly) and Mrs. Kingsbury that Calvin Cutler is also one and is a relation of mine . . . . .

Your ever devoted husband and father
EPHRAIM CUTLER

(Unsigned letter)   May 27, 1837

I have scarcely noted anything that has occurred since my arrival here and for essence can only say that until yesterday I was unpleasantly situated in a fourth floor loft in a small room with few conveniences & I am now on the second floor in a room with Mr. Roberts, Mr. C. Cutler and Mr. Dolbeare, pleasant companions.

The doings of the Assembly (General Assembly of the Presbyterian Church) with the interesting debates which will be reported by that excellent man, Mr. Stansbury, formerly a Presbyterian minister and one of the best reporters ever yet in the U. S.

Baltimore & Ohio Railroad
Barber, David
Barker, Joseph
Bridges, Ohio River
Cutler, Ephraim
Cutler, Mrs. Ephraim (2),
  (Sally Parker)
Cutler, William P.
Duncan, E.
Emerson, Caleb
Ewing, Thomas
Garrett, ————————
Gates, Beman
Gill, M.
Hildreth, Samuel P.
Hopkins, Johns
Kennedy, A.
Latrobe, Benjamin H.
McLane, Louis
Maps

Mills, John
Mosely, Thomas W. H.
Nye, Arius
Nye, William S.
Parker, Sally (Mrs. Ephraim Cutler, 2)
Shipman, Charles
Stone, Augustus
Tidbull, Alex
Trimble, Isaac
Trimble, John
Tucker, Henry St. George
Vinton, Samuel
Virginia, State of
Walker, A. B.
Ward, Nahum
Washington County Railroad Committee
Wilson, John, Jr.
Wilson, Noah L.

CHAPTER 13

THE CUTLERS AND ANTI-SLAVERY

Ephraim Cutler and his son, William P. Cutler lived according to the precepts for the government of the Northwest Territory, the Ordinance of 1787, which stated in Article VI that "There shall be neither slavery nor involuntary servitude in the said territory," and the second article of the Ohio Constitution of 1802, devised by Ephraim Cutler, which forbade slavery within the limits of the new state. Also, as a member of the Ohio Legislature in the early 1820's, he was the leader against the proposed Black Laws.

William P. Cutler, throughout his legislative career, both in the Ohio Legislature and in Congress, often spoke out against the system. In the years before the War between the States, there began the practice of encouraging slaves to escape into the Northern states and Canada, a practice that became known as the "Underground Railroad." Since the Cutler home was by the Ohio River, escaping slaves often crossed the River into the community.

One notable event of this kind occurred on the night of July 9, 1845 when six slaves of John H. Howard at Washington's Bottom, Wood County, Virginia, crossed the river near Blennerhasset Island, and were met by three Belpre citizens who were to be their "Underground conductors" to the next station in Ohio. The so called 'conductors' were arrested by Parkersburg law officers and were lodged in the Parkersburg jail and held without bond, a case that became known as the Parkersburg Slave Case. The affair reached the halls of the Ohio State Legislature of which William P. Cutler was a member and even the high courts of the United States.

The Cutler Collection of Letters and Documents, now in the Dawes Memorial Library of Marietta College, includes nine letters which pertain to the period of the Underground Railroad. The list of the names of the correspondents follows:

Bartley, Gov. Mordacai
Birney, William

Borden, Stanton
Cutler, Ephraim

CHAPTER 14

THE WARREN PRESBYTERIAN CHURCH

The early history of the Warren Presbyterian Church in Warren Township was closely allied with the family of Ephraim Cutler. Besides helping to found the religious organization, the family was among its most generous supporters for over half of a century.

The organization grew out of the religious desires of the settlers of the community for a church home. Before the founding, there had been loosely organized Sabbath Schools held in the homes of the leading residents, and occasional sermons by the clergy of Belpre and Marietta, and by itinerant missionaries enroute to their assignments farther to the West.

The organization of the religious society dates back to the winter of 1824-1825 when two missionaries from the Connecticut Missionary Society, on their way down the Ohio river, became stranded by an ice jamb. These dedicated men, named Chamberlain and West, resolute in their missions, asked if they might visit the homes of the community with a view to establishing a church society. They were welcomed during their stay of a few weeks and thus became the founders of the society.

Ephraim Cutler, though not a member of any church, but true to his religious background and home surroundings, joined in the efforts, which after four years, 1824-1828 resulted in a Presbyterian church of the Athens Presbytery. Cutler was among the first group of the membership.

Beman, Rev. W.
Birge, Louis M.
Burgess, Rev. Dyer
Coomes, H.
Curtis, Walter
Cutler, Daniel C.
Cutler, Ephraim
Cutler, William P.
Edwards, J. S.
Harlow, C. B.
Humphreys, E. T.
Humphreys, Isaac
Humphreys, Mary
Kingsbury, Addison

Little, Jacob
Merwin, C. H.
Ministerial Land Funds
Newton, Oren
Presbyterian General Assembly
Rosseter, William D.
Seiss, Rev. Joseph A.
Slocomb, John M.
Slocomb, William
Smith, George, Jr.
Smith, Rev. W. A.
Warren Presbyterian Church
Warren Sabbath School
Union Society

CHAPTER 15

THE WESTERN LIBRARY ASSOCIATION

The early settlers in the outlying areas of the Ohio Company's Purchase, especially those isolated by miles of distance away from the settlements along the Ohio and Muskingum rivers, found themselves in the midst of dense forests abounding in every variety of wild animal native to the region. Having come from New England, where life had developed to a high degree of civilization, they soon realized that their success in spite of their isolation would depend upon their physical efforts and ingenuities for obtaining food and clothing and other necessities for their existence.

For food, it was necessary to fell the trees and clear space for garden plots for vegetables, and to enlarge the clearing for planting grain. For their clothing and meats, they hunted the predatory wild animals. Every effort that they exerted was to overcome the handicaps and turn them into assets. In addition to physical obstacles, the pioneers were further isolated by the lack of reading materials. There was irregular mail service, and in the early years only the occasional traveler who would venture into the area. Therefore, the question was how to make some obstacle into an asset, to turn some marketable product into money for the purchase of books and other reading materials.

In the Amesville community, there was but one newspaper subscription, and each issue came three months after publication. Finally a traveler came to the settlement and was apprised of the situation. He related that there was a rapidly expanding fur trade in the seaboard markets, founded by John Jacob Astor, and that fur prices were at a premium.

Why not, they reasoned, turn the obstacle of predatory fur bearing animals into an asset since almost every male settler, with his ever-trusty rifle, was bringing in furs for which there was no market? Accordingly, a Library Association was organized. Shares were sold for $2.50 each to provide the capital, with a fee of 25 cents a year for use of the Library. Ephraim Cutler purchased four shares, Silvanus Ames, who had come from the Belpre settlement where there was a circulating library, joined in the project by purchasing two shares. The total number of shares sold was 34.

The organization was not completed until 1801, when one of the settlers, Samuel Brown, began preparations for a wagon trip to Boston. He took along a supply of furs, and while in Boston, he purchased books for the price of $73.50. He had found a ready market for furs both in New York and Boston.

The library organization became a reality in 1804 when the Ohio Legislature gave it a charter as the Western Library Association. In after-years, since furs had been the origin, the Library was popularly known as the "Coonskin" Library. It was antedated by only three other library associations, The Belpre Farmers Library, 1796, The Cincinnati Public Library, February 13, 1802, and the Erie Literary Society of Trumbull County, April 16, 1803.

The books accumulated by the "Coonskin" library grew to several hundred volumes, a considerable number for what was considered a small isolated community in that early period. Many years later the Library was divided, and a part was taken to Dover Township in Athens County where a number of the original stockholders had moved. The portion retained by the Ames settlement was sold in 1860 or 1861 to J. G. Glazier, A. W. Glazier, and E. H. Brawley. This portion was afterward sold to William P. Cutler of Washington County, who at his death in 1889, willed the remainder of the books to his daughter, Miss Sarah J. Cutler of Marietta. Miss Cutler, some years before her death in 1933, donated the Library to the Ohio Historical Society where it is now on display—a monument to the ingenuity of the once isolated settlers in a remote small community one hundred and sixty years ago.

CHAPTER 16

EPHRAIM CUTLER — MISCELLANY

The Collection, gathered under the subject of Miscellany, embraces Ephraim Cutler's account books, Historical articles of the early years of the Ohio Company settlement, copies of speeches, the founding of the grindstone industry in Warren Township and the years of his postmastership of Constitution, Ohio, from his appointment in 1842 until his retirement from active life.

The Collection is a part of the Cutler Collection of Letters and Documents housed in the Dawes Memorial Library of Marietta College. The following is the list of names of persons mentioned therein:

Curtis, Walter
Cushing, Nathaniel
Cutler, Clarissa (Mrs. James S. Walton)
Cutler, Ephraim, Historical Discourses
Cutler, Ephraim, Memoranda
Cutler, Jervis
Cutler, Julia P.
Cutler, Manasseh
Cutler, William
Cutler, William P.
Dana, Joseph
Dexter, Timothy
Dodge, John
Eddy, Henry
Elkins, Henry
Everett, Moses
Ewing, Thomas
Fearing, Paul
Federal Creek
Ford, William
Foster, Peregrine
Foster, Polly
Friend, Hannah
Friend, John
Friend, Lucy
Gates, Beman
Graves, Asa
Gray, Walter
Green, John
Green, Ray
Greene, Griffin
Grosvenor, Robert
Halibut, Eleazer
Halliday, Samuel
Harris, John
Hartshorn, Thomas
Hatch, Elijah
Henderson, Hugh
Herrick, John
Hicky, James
Hildreth, Samuel P.
Home, The Old Stone House
Howe, Sampson
Howes, John H.
Humphrey, Joseph C.

Isham, Joshua
Ives, Thomas
Kanawah Salines
Kerr, Hamilton
Kip, D. W.
Lafayette, Marquis de
Laslie, David
Linscot, Mary
Lippitt, Joseph
Loomis, L.
Lummis, John
McBride, William
McClure, Andrew
McClure, Harry
McClure, W. D.
Mail Routes, U. S.
Maltbie, Benjamin
Manning, C.
Marietta Historical Association
Mays, Col. John
Miller, Robert
Mills, Dorothy Webster
Mills, John
Moore, Col. James
Napier, Robert
Newton, Oren
Northwest Territory First Court
Nye, Anselm T.
O'Brien, John
Ohio Bible Society
Ohio Company
Ohio River Floods
Ohio River Keelboats
Ohio River, Kerr's Island
Ohio, State of, Census Statistics
Ohio, State of, Legislature
Oliver, Robert
Parker, Billy
Parker, William
Parsons, Enoch
Parsons, Samuel
Pearce, Samuel
Pearse, Samuel
Pearse, Sarah
Pearse, Stephen
Poole, Fitch
Putnam, William R.

CHAPTER 17

EPHRAIM CUTLER — THE CLOSING YEARS

Ephraim Cutler, as is recorded by his daughter, Julia Perkins Cutler, spent the closing years of his life quietly in the OLD STONE HOUSE. William P. Cutler, his only surviving son, handled the business of the family as the worthy successor to a most admirable father. In 1850 Julia wrote in her diary on her father's eighty-third birthday "except for his deafness he might be thought fifteen years younger . . .". "Pa came home this evening having ridden through snow and wind—twenty-eight miles." Ephraim Cutler lived patiently and wisely until his death, July 8, 1853.

The funeral service was conducted by the Rev. Ebenezer B. Andrews, who also conducted the burial rites in the Gravel Bank cemetery in Warren Township, beside the graves of his two wives, Leah Atwood Cutler, 1768-1807 and Sally Parker Cutler, 1777-1846, and his son, Manasseh, 1810-1822.

The epitaph on his tombstone, now partially indistinct, records the following:

EPHRAIM CUTLER
Son of Rev. Manasseh Cutler, L.L.D.
Born at Edgartown, Mass.
April 13, 1767
He emigrated to the Territory
Northwest of the Ohio, 1795
was appointed Judge
of the Court of Common Pleas
and of the Quarter Sessions, 1797
was a member of the
Territorial Legislature, 1801
and of the Convention which
formed the Constitution
of the State of Ohio, 1802
He afterwards filled many places of
usefulness and honor and labored to promote
education, religion and true freedom
He died July 8, 1853
aged 86 years

CHAPTER 18

THE CUTLER FAMILY LETTERS

The Cutler Collection of Letters and Documents in the Dawes
Memorial Library at Marietta College contains many family letters
of the Cutler and Dawes families. The following are the names of
the correspondents along with some of the principal subjects con-
tained therein:

Amesville Farm
Barber, Elizabeth
Beecher, Lyman
Bennett, John Cook
Civil War Scrapbook
Cutler, Clarissa (Mrs. James S.
  Walton)
Cutler, Ephraim
Cutler, Mrs. Ephraim (2)
  (Sally Parker)
Cutler, Maj. Jervis
Cutler, Gen. Joseph
Cutler, Julia Perkins
Cutler, Manasseh
Cutler, Manasseh, (1810-1822)
Cutler, Mary, (Mrs. Gulliver Dean)
Cutler, Sarah Jane,
  (Mrs. Henry Dawes)
Cutler, Temple, I
Cutler, Maj. Temple, II
Cutler, William P.
Cutler, Mrs. William P.
  (Elizabeth Williamson Voris)
Dawes, Ephraim C.
Dawes, Lucinda Catherine (Kate)
  (Mrs. Samuel A. McLean)
Dawes, Henry
Dawes, Mrs. Henry
  (Sarah Jane Cutler)
Dawes, Sarah Jane,
  (Mrs. John H. Shedd)
Dean, Mrs. Gulliver, (Mary Cutler)

Farm Affairs
Federal Creek Floods
Goodale, Lincoln
Granville Female Seminary
Greene, Mary
Harrison, William H.
Hildreth, Marion
Kilbourne, James
Kingsbury, Addison
Loco-Foco Party
McLean, Mrs. Samuel A.
  (Lucinda Catherine (Kate) Dawes)
Marietta & Cincinnati Railroad
Marietta Collegiate Institute
Mills, John
Nebraska Lands
Ohio (Second) Constitutional Con-
  vention
Ohio University
Parker, Sally (Mrs. Ephraim
  Cutler, 2)
Shedd, Mrs. John H.
  (Sarah Jane Dawes)
Stone, Augustus
Stone quarry affairs
Torrey, A.
Voris, Elizabeth Williamson
  (Mrs. William P. Cutler)
Walton, Mrs. James S.
  (Clarissa Cutler)
Whitney, Sarah

CHAPTER 19

THE PARKER FAMILY

Ephraim Cutler's second wife, to whom he was married on April 13, 1808, was Miss Sally Parker, a descendant of a prominent New England family which had settled there in 1669. She was the daughter of William Parker, who with his family started to the Ohio Country in 1788, but because of the Indian hostilities spent several years on the banks of the Monongahela River, arriving in 1795, after a hazardous journey, at their original destination where Parker was a shareholder in The Ohio Company. He settled his family in an area later known as Meigs County.

William Parker, a carpenter and cabinet maker had purchased a small farm and also worked at his trade while sojourning on the Monongahela River. Sally, the third of nine children, was born at Newburyport, Massachusetts, in 1777, and died at the Cutler home at Constitution, Ohio, in 1846. As the wife of Ephraim Cutler, she was the mother of five children, as follows:

> Sarah, 1809-1896, the wife of Henry Dawes
> Manasseh, 1810-1822
> William Parker, 1812-1889
> Julia Perkins, 1814-1904
> Clarissa Warner, 1816-1874

LETTERS AND DOCUMENTS:
1. Letters of Sally Parker Cutler to Ephraim Cutler
2. The Parker Family Letters

CHAPTER 20

THE SHIPMAN FAMILY

Among the allied ancestral lines of the Cutler-Dawes families was that of Shipman, a name which had been prominent in Connecticut as far back as 1667. The first progenitor to settle in the Northwest Territory was Joshua Shipman, (1767-1823,) who, having made a trip of inspection, in 1789, of the opportunities for a livelihood in the new country, migrated, with his wife, the former Sybil Chapman, and their three year old son, Charles, to Marietta in October, 1790. Mrs. Shipman was the daughter of an earlier settler, Levi Chapman, who had entered land in Salem Township in Washington County.

The first residence of the Shipman's was a log cabin in the part of Marietta, then known as Liberty Hill within sight of the Campus Martius fortifications, to which they moved because of the increasing Indian troubles.

Joshua was a carpenter and house builder, a trade which he had followed for some years, and in Marietta he immediately found a growing demand for his talents following the conclusion of the Indian War. Among the edifices that he built in Marietta were the

Muskingum Academy and the Old Two Horn (Congregational) Church which were landmarks in the town for many years.

After coming to Marietta, eight other children were born, Harriett, who died in infancy; William Henry, 1793-1829; Frederick, 1795-1839; Joshua, 1797-1829; Elizabeth, 1800-1830; Julia, Mrs. Nathaniel Holden, 1802-1872; Maria, Mrs. Isaac Shook, 1804-1865; Samuel, 1807-1880; and Joseph Chapman, 1810-1829. Two of the sons, Charles and Samuel, throughout their lives were prominent and influential citizens in Athens, Marietta and Gallipolis.

Charles Shipman, the eldest son, 1787-1860, spent his boyhood with his family in Marietta, helping his father in his building operations. He was a pupil in the Muskingum Academy during the first years of its existence, 1800-1801 under the tutelage of the first teacher and principal, David Putnam. In his boyhood years he was employed as a clerk in the drug store of Dr. Jabez True and later on in the drug store of Dr. Increase Mathews in Putnam (Zanesville). A note in his diary, found many years later, states that he was a pupil in Marietta's first Sunday School, organized by Mary Lake. Another note in his diary, 1808, told of a trip back to the old Shipman home in Saybrook, Connecticut, and of walking most of the way. He was then 21 years of age.

Soon after his return to Marietta, he was married to Frances White Dana of Belpre and went to live in Gallipolis where he engaged in the mercantile business. While in Gallipolis, a son, William Charles Shipman, 1812-1836, was born and soon thereafter, bereavement came in the death of his wife.

Later in 1812 he went, by chance, to Athens to a general muster of the militia, and being attracted to the village, he decided to return and open a store. During the War of 1812, as a militiaman in the Company of General Edward W. Tupper, he received three promotions, first an adjutancy, followed by a commission as a major, and finally to a colonel.

In 1814, he was married to Joanna Herrick Bartlett, the daughter of Henry and Betsey (Corey) Bartlett. They became the parents of five children, three daughters, Joanna Frances, (1815-1903) who became the wife of Sala Bosworth in Marietta, Betsey Sybil, (1816-1895), who became Mrs. Beman Gates, also of Marietta, and Charlotte Orphana, (1818-1827), and two sons, Henry Bartlett (1821-1902), and John Bartlett, (1823-1906).

Mary Beman Gates, the daughter of Beman Gates and Betsey Sybil (Shipman) Gates, became the wife of General Rufus R. Dawes, and the mother of the Dawes family; Charles Gates Dawes, Rufus Cutler Dawes, Beman Gates Dawes, Henry Manasseh, Mary, (Mrs. Arthur G. Beach) and Betsey, (Mrs. Harry B. Hoyt.)

Charles Shipman, with his family lived in Athens, Ohio, for a quarter of a century, where he established a large mercantile business. He was a founder of the Presbyterian Church of Athens and a leader in the temperance movement. A total abstainer, he was one of the first store keepers to ban the sale of liquor from his establishment. He was also instrumental in founding the first agricultural society in Ohio. His home in Athens, built in the 1820's is still standing, (1962).

In 1837, Charles Shipman, moved with his family to Marietta where he joined in a partnership with his brother, Samuel, (1807-1880) in a mercantile business at Front and Greene Streets.

Samuel Shipman received his education, first in Muskingum Academy and later on in Ohio University. Samuel lived throughout his entire life in Marietta, becoming, like his brother, Charles, had in Athens, one of the leading citizens of Marietta. In 1855 he was elected Treasurer of Marietta College, an office which he held for 12 years. In 1859 he was elected to the Board of Trustees of Marietta College and continued to serve until his death in 1880.

The Shipman Letters and Documents, now a part of the Marietta College Archives, cover a long period of American history dating from the seventeenth century in New England to the late 1800's in Ohio. They reveal a considerable portion of local history in Ohio, Marietta, Gallipolis, Athens and Zanesville, where business and social activities were centered.

Adams, D.
Allen, D. Howe
Allen & Grant
American Sunday School Union
Ashton, Hetty Bartlett
Atwood & Company
Backus, A. L.
Backus, L.
Baker, Seth
Baltimore & Ohio Railroad
Barber, Levi

Barker, Joseph, Jr.
Barstow, L. S.
Bartlett, Henrietta
Bartlett, Henry
Bartlett, Joanna Herrick
    (Mrs. Charles Shipman, 2)
Bartlett, John
Bartlett, Rebecca G.
Beardsley, Frances
Beckley & Shipman

Bevan, John
Bingham, Luther G.
Blake, Bigelow
Blakely, Abraham
Bosworth, Joseph D.
Bosworth, J. G.
Bosworth, Joseph W.
Bosworth, Sala
Brown, C. P.
Brown, Charles H.
Brown, William B.
Cating, John
Chapman, Samuel
Chapman, Levi
Chidlaw, N.
Clemens, Samuel
Cone, Mary
Conn, James
Cooksey, Levi
Creed, John
Crist, J. B.
Creston, Wistar & Co.
Cromwell & Dobbin
Culver, C. G.
Cushing, N. L.
Cushing, S. L.
Cutler, Daniel
Cutler, Ephraim
Cutler, William P.
Dana, Caroline
Dana, Eliza
Dana, Frances White
    (Mrs. Charles Shipman, 1)
Dana, Joseph
Dana, Louisa
Davidson, Thomas
deSteiguer, R.
Doan, Archibald L.
Dodge, Oliver
Dorr, John
Dorrance, William L.
Doughty, George W.
Dunbar, Elon
Dunbar & Co.
Dunbar, Brooks & Dunning
Dunlevy, George
Emlen, Sam W.
Everett, Daniel

Everett, Eunice
Foster, Eben
Francis, James
Francis, Thomas
Gilbert, Augusta P.
Gilbert, Susan L.
Gilman, Joseph
Goddard & Converse
Gondrum, Martha
Griffin, Asahel
Griffin, Samuel J.
Hale, S. K.
Hamson, James
Haraden, Eliza
Harris, Thaddeus
Haskell, A. H.
Hatch, E.
Hay, Henry
Hayward, Solomon
Henry, John
Herrick, Bertha
Hildreth, Samuel P.
Hodgeman, Stephen A.
Howard, Joseph
Humphreys, Joseph B.
Hunt, J. E.
Hutchinson, William
Ingersoll, Mrs.
Jackson, Eleanor
Jaquith, Sarah
Knowles, Lucy
Lafore, A.
Landreth, D. & C.
Lanham, James
Lanham, Susan D.
Lanham, Susanna
Le Peyre, Farrouth & Co.
Lewis, John E.
Linsley, Joel B.
List, John
Lord, Abner
McFarland, James
Mansion House, Marietta
Marsh, E.
Marshall, Thomas W.
Mathews, Increase
Meacham, Mrs. Anna
Menager, Romain

Menager, S. B.
Merrill, A.
Mills, John
Moore, Jonas
Morgan, D. T.
Morris, C. A.
Neff, Addison
Northwestern Bank of Virginia
Nye, Arius
Nye, Horace
Nye, Ichabod
Ohio Mutual Fire Insurance Co.
Ohio University
Palmer, W.
Peirce, Thomas
Perkins, Eliphaz
Perkins, Ruth
Pickering, Samuel
Porter, William
Powell, O. S.
Pratt, Timothy
Preston, William
Price, Mrs. Sarah B.
Prince, Mrs. Joanna
Purdy, M. A.
Reed & Morgan
Reed, C. M.
Reed, George M.
Rice, Asa
Rice, Theresa
Root, N.
Scovil & Co.
Shipman, Ansel
Shipman, Betsey
Shipman, Charles
Shipman, Mrs. Charles, 1,
    (Frances White Dana)
Shipman, Mrs. Charles, 2,
    (Joanna Herrick Bartlett)
Shipman, Elizabeth
Shipman, Henry B.
Shipman, Joanna F.

Shipman, John B.
Shipman, Joseph C.
Shipman, Joshua
Shipman, Julia
Shipman, Lucinda
Shipman, Maria
Shipman, Samuel
Shipman, W. C.
Shipman, W. H.
Skillington, Thomas
Skinner, D. C.
Smith & Brothers
Spaulding, O. C.
Spencer, D. B.
Spencer, J.
Spenser, William
Sperry, Jared
Stedman, Abel
Steele, Donnally & Steele
Steele, Ellen W.
Stewart, Ezra
Stone, Augustus
Stone, Augustus Israel
Stone, Bosworth & Welch
Strickland, William
Sullivan, John W.
Thacher, Peter
Trimble, Carey A.
Truman & Smith
Tufts, Susanna
Tupper, Edward W.
Vinton, Abel
Walker, William
Warner, N. O.
Westcott, Samuel A.
Whipple, E. A.
Whitney, James
Wickham, Thomas B.
Wilson, Noah L.
Wilson, William & Co.
Woodbridge, Dudley
Woodbridge, George M.

W. P. Cutler

CHAPTER 21

WILLIAM PARKER CUTLER

William Parker Cutler, the second son of Ephraim and Sally (Parker) Cutler was born in 1812 at the Cutler Homestead in Warren Township, Washington County, Ohio. Throughout his adult life he became known as one of the leading men in the State of Ohio in the fields of industry, politics, education and religion.

His education began early in his boyhood. His mother, herself a scholar, directed his primary education through his early years and both his father and mother provided him with books, newspaper and other educational materials far in excess of those found in the average pioneer household. He was prepared for college in the Academy of Ohio University, of which his father was a trustee, and in 1829, he began his college work in that institution. At the close of his junior year, he was forced to withdraw because of ill health, a situation which often recurred throughout the whole of his busy life.

Returning to the farm in the hope that outdoor life might help him to regain his health, he met with disappointment over the slowness of recovery. The following year, 1834 he sought the curative benefits of travel by a leisurely journey on horseback through the states of Virginia and North Carolina for a visit with a former classmate who was a physician in Mecklinburg of the latter state. In his diary of the trip, he recorded an item of his stay at the White Sulphur Springs Inn, "Spent a week, lodging and horsefeed, $8.25."

On returning from his North Carolina sojourn, with his health greatly improved, he assisted his father on the farm and in small business enterprises, among them, the grindstone industry, which had been founded by his father and a neighbor, that was to continue through their successors for nearly a century.

In the late 1830's, he entered a new phase of his life, that of a public speaker and orator, the training for which began in the literary societies of his Alma Mater. He soon, by the effectiveness of his public speeches, attracted the attention of the leaders of the Whig

Party in Ohio and within a year thereafter, entered actively into political life. In 1842, he was nominated as a candidate for the Ohio House of Representatives, but was defeated at the election. In 1844, he again became a candidate for the Legislature and was successful. Before the close of the session, he had become the floor leader for his Party. In 1845 and again in 1846, he was re-elected, and in the latter session, was chosen speaker of the House of Representatives.

In 1848, he was nominated to represent the Congressional District, composed of Washington, Morgan and Perry counties for the United States Congress, but failed to win the election. A year later he was chosen to represent Washington County in the Convention for revising the Constitution of the State of Ohio.

In 1845, he had begun another of the important phases of his career, the railroad industry, then non-existent in Ohio. In the legislative session of 1845-1846 he had been influential in securing a charter for the Belpre & Cincinnati Railroad, a line that was being projected from Marietta to Cincinnati. From that year and throughout the following quarter of a century, he had a vision that the commercial growth of the State of Ohio for trade and industry could be realized only in the construction of railroads that would transport the farm and industrial products to the markets of the rapidly growing cities.

In 1847, he was elected to the directorship of the Belpre & Cincinnati Railroad, and in 1850 was chosen as its president. In the meantime the name of the railroad had been changed to the Marietta & Cincinnati Railroad.

On his entry into railroad operations, Cutler soon found that the first obstacle to be overcome was the acquisition of capital funds, a condition of economics that was to harass him and his partners throughout his railroad building career. Financial depressions were ever recurring, the first in Cutler's career in the early 1850's in Ohio during the construction of the Marietta & Cincinnati line and its extension northward on the Ohio side of the Ohio River toward a connection with the Pennsylvania Railroad. The construction of the railroad toward Cincinnati progressed, but the projected line northward from Marietta, with only twelve miles of surveying and grading, came to an end.

However, despite the financial conditions of the economy, the construction work on the Marietta & Cincinnati Railroad was continued and by March, 1857, the trains were running on schedule.

In the meantime, Cutler suffered another breakdown in health in which he was forced to surrender his presidency to another director, Noah L. Wilson. He again, sought relief by travel, touring into the Middle West as far as Iowa and Minnesota.

On his return, with his health partially restored, Cutler resumed his activities with the directors of the Marietta & Cincinnati Railroad in solving its financial difficulties and was soon rewarded with trains again running on schedule, with some exceptions as an occasional train wreck, washouts, and the collapsing of tunnels. But more capital was necessary, which he sought by traveling to Baltimore for an interview with the officials of the Baltimore & Ohio Railroad for the consolidation of the two railroads on a temporary basis, in order that a connecting line would be built from Moore's Junction to Belpre. The Baltimore & Ohio directors refused to grant additional capital.

He then returned to Marietta and organized a corporation of local capitalists which was to be known as the Union Railroad to connect Moore's Junction and Belpre, so as to join the Marietta and Belpre communities with a rail line, and thereby connect it with the Marietta & Cincinnati road. The venture was completed, with trains running in 1859.

In the same year, Cutler gave up, partially, his railroad activities and turned his attention to politics. Having been a "Free Soil" Whig, he hailed the dawn of a new day in the formation of the Republican Party, the organic idea of which was its opposition to the extension of slavery. In 1860, by a plurality of 733 votes he was elected to the 37th Congress of the United States from the Ohio District composed of Washington, Morgan and Muskingum Counties, and taking his seat on July 4th, 1861 when the Congress was called for an extra session.

Along with his Congressional duties, Cutler remained as vice-president of the Marietta & Cincinnati Railroad. While under the strain of his twofold responsibilities, he was stricken with typhoid fever, but recovered sufficiently to return to his Congressional seat a few days after the opening of the session in December, 1861.

In Congress, he achieved national prominence for his stand on anti-slavery. His opposition was expressed in a speech delivered on April 23, 1862, the preamble to which was:

1. It is the right and duty of Congress to destroy every enemy that threatens the National life.

2. Slavery is an enemy; therefore it is the right of Congress to destroy it.

The speech, along with his oratorical qualities, again reminiscent of his literary society days in Ohio University, was widely commended in both Northern newspapers and personal letters from influential men such as Alphonso Taft, Lewis Tappan and Horace Greeley, and it was regarded in Congress as a step toward the freeing of the slaves. President Lincoln's Proclamation of September 22, 1862, is said to have been a result in that national opinion had been brought to a climax for the emancipation of the slaves in the states engaged in the rebellion.

Cutler was again nominated for Congress in 1862, but was defeated in the election, being succeeded by the Democratic nominee. However his influence in naming presidential appointments for Ohio continued for more than a year following the close of his term.

Returning to Ohio and to his home at Constitution, Cutler renewed his activity as vice-president of the Marietta & Cincinnati Railroad which in the early years of the War had become more solvent with the increased traffic occasioned by war transportation of troops and freight. In July of 1863, he rendered noble service in supervising his employees along with the Ohio militia in protecting the railroad from the raiders led by General John H. Morgan, by placing them in strategic locations, and thus preventing any cessation of traffic through the two terrifying weeks of the enemy in Southern Ohio.

Beside his vice-presidency of the Railroad, he operated the Old Home Farm at Constitution along with other farming interests in the Amesville neighborhood. But railroad affairs occupied most of his time and attention. While in Congress, he had been instrumental in securing a Federal charter authorizing the construction of a railroad bridge across the Ohio River from Parkersburg to Belpre. Such a bridge would connect the Baltimore & Ohio Railroad with the already built Union Railroad from Belpre to Moore's Junction, thus eliminating the transporting of railroad cars by ferry up the Ohio River to Moore's Junction, and thereby improving the service westward to Cincinnati and the west.

Also, with the knowledge, provided by geologists and engineers, of the rich coal and iron deposits in Southeastern Ohio and in the Hocking Valley and Sunday Creek regions northward towards Columbus, he planned a network of branch lines that would greatly improve the outlets toward central Ohio.

Again the lack of capital funds proved an obstacle and he was forced to withdraw his efforts for railroad construction. However, some years afterward, other capitalists built a rail line which for years was known as the Columbus & Hocking Valley, following the plans which Cutler had made a decade before.

In the meantime, the directors of the Marietta & Cincinnati Railroad were harassed in their efforts to raise capital funds and the Baltimore & Ohio Railroad took advantage of the financial plight and gradually took over the line, thus forcing Cutler to resign his vice-presidency. In a letter written to one of his friends on May 16, 1868, he wrote: "I have severed my connections with the M. & C. Railroad."

Cutler's ambitions for railroad building were by no means at an end. In 1868, he set out to organize another railroad, a line that would extend northward from Marietta toward a connection with the Pennsylvania Railroad in Central Ohio, a road to be known as the Marietta and Pittsburgh Railroad. He was made president of the new line, and began at once for its construction. Again, he and his associates were confronted with the lack of capital which resulted in receiverships and reorganizations. However, Cutler had the satisfaction again, of knowing that on January 19, 1872, trains were running from Marietta to Caldwell, Ohio, and in another two years they were reaching a junction with the Pennsylvania lines at Newcomerstown and Canal Dover.

The next stage of Cutler's railroad building career began in 1869 when he became associated with a new corporation of directors, some of them his former associates in the Marietta & Cincinnati Railroad. He and his associates turned their ambitions westward, into Indiana and Illinois and progressed with inadequate capital for another network of rail lines including the towns of Crawfordsville, Indiana, Pana and Shawneetown, Illinois, and other towns situated in the agricultural and coal mining regions of the two states. Again the raising of capital funds became a problem, and he was faced by the national economic depression of 1873, which found him and his associates with heavy loans and only partially finished construction. Therefore, at the age of sixty-one he gave up most of his property and was without sufficient money and credit for further railroad construction. So severe was his lack of funds that he sold THE OLD STONE HOUSE and moved to Marietta where he spent the remainder of his life.

The final chapter in William P. Cutler's railroad building career came in 1884. The Baltimore & Ohio Railroad, operating under the name of Cincinnati, Washington & Baltimore, had built what was known as the "Short Line" from Belpre toward Athens to connect with the old Marietta & Cincinnati Railroad, thereby abandoning the "Old Line" through Washington County from Marietta to Big Run. At the organization meeting in Marietta, held April 29, 1884, Cutler explained from the statistics which he had gathered, that the "Old Line" should run through an area in Washington and Athens counties, which if properly developed would be a great source of trade for Marietta. It would connect also with coal and oil resources in the Federal Creek Valley. Soon the organization was completed, with Cutler elected to the presidency, serving as such until 1887. The name of the corporation was the Marietta Mineral Railway Company. He wrote in his reminiscences that "No other achievement of his life gave him more satisfaction than this last public work in which he was engaged."

The last of Cutler's business career came in the late 1870's and early 1880's when he spent a good part of his time in Iowa with a relative in a small commercial business and speculation in lands.

In the final years of his life, he turned to the historical research on his family and ancestors and in the history of the State of Ohio. He was active in 1876 in organizing the local celebration of the Centennial of the Declaration of Independence. He was also active in the founding of the Ohio Archaeological and Historical Society and in writing articles pertaining to the Northwest Territory Ordinance and the migrations of the early pioneers. He was also the chairman of the organization for the Centennial Celebration of the Founding of Marietta, which preceded by only a few months his death in 1889.

No sketch of the life of William Parker Cutler can be complete without mentioning his adherence to his family traditions, the purchase of the remaining books of the "Coonskin" or Western Library Association of which his father was one of the founders, and the

Warren Township Presbyterian Church of his neighborhood, and his forty years as a Trustee of Marietta College. His most monumental work of writing and publishing was the Life, Journal and Correspondence of his grandfather, Manasseh Cutler, written with the collaboration of his sister, Julia Perkins Cutler, and published in 1888, and the Life and Times of Ephraim Cutler, also with the collaboration of his sister. He did not live to see the book in print as his death occurred the year before publication of the volume.

CHAPTER 22

WILLIAM P. CUTLER AND HIS EDUCATION

AT OHIO UNIVERSITY

William P. Cutler, as stated in the preceding chapter, received his preparatory and college education at Ohio University. While there, he made a large number of friends with whom he corresponded for several years. He was forced, because of ill health to withdraw in 1833 while a member of the Junior Class. Some years later, in the 1840's he was awarded the degree of Master of Arts, as stated in the citation, "for distinguishing himself in the walks of science, virtue and usefulness." He was elected to the Board of Trustees, but never served.

The names of his principal correspondents are herein listed, and their letters are to be found in the Cutler Collection of the Dawes Memorial Library of Marietta College.

Brice, Benjamin
Brown, Archibald G.
Chidlaw, B. C.
Cutler, Charles, son of Ephraim
Dickey, Theophilus L.
McFarland, William

Ohio University Literary Societies
Olds, Chauncey
Patton, Joseph W.
Wilson, Lafayette
Wilson, W. M.
Young, W. H.

CHAPTER 23

WILLIAM PARKER CUTLER

MISCELLANEOUS CORRESPONDENCE 1835-1889

The Correspondence of William P. Cutler occupies a large portion of this volume, and is listed in the several categories of his lifetime activities, his association with Ohio University, his political life and business career. The letters and documents are herein classified under the titles: Ohio University, the Ohio Legislature, and the Ohio Constitutional Convention; Second, the Building of the Marietta & Cincinnati Railroad, Congress and the War Years, Railroad Construction after 1865 and in the later period of his life, and the Centennials of 1876 and 1888.

The Letters and Documents of William P. Cutler are in the Manuscript Collection in the Dawes Memorial Library of Marietta College.

The following is a list of his correspondents, selected from 1835 to his death in 1889:

Addy, William	Crouch, C.
Anderson, Charles	Cutler, D. C.
Andrews, Ebenezer B.	Cutler, Manasseh
Andrews, Israel W.	Cutler, Waldo
Bailey, Augustus	Cutler, William P.
Bay, Amin	Dana, George
Bizer, John	Dickey, A. S.
Bosworth, Sala	Earl, W. C.
Brown, Archibald G.	Fay, Catherine A.
Brown, Henry T.	Finch, Lewis
Brown, John P.	Fisher, George S.
Bukey, Van R.	Gillet, James
Burgess, Dyer	Glazier, A. B.
Chamberlain, L. W.	Goodman, F. S.
Cheedham, Barton	Greene, N. M.
Coles, Daniel R.	Grow, George B.

Gurley, William H.
Hall & Tooker
Halliday, S.
Harnden Express Co.
Hayes, Rutherford B.
Hornaus, J. S.
Howes, J. H.
Hyer, Jacob
Jaynes, A. D.
Johnson, W. W.
Lacey, Eliza
Lewis, A. H.
Leykins, Stanley
Lindley, H. B.
Linsley, Joel H.
McClintick & Smith
McClure, H. O.
McKay, J. A.
Means, John
Means, Thomas
Mower, Mrs. E.
Merwin, Charles H.
Moore, T. W.
Morrow, Jeremiah

Norris, G. W.
Nye, D. S.
Ohio Republican Committee
Ohio State Bank, Logan Branch
Ordinance of 1787
Parker, E. W.
Parker, N.
Patterson, John
Plants, T. A.
Plumley, B. S.
Plumly, Joseph W.
Putnam, William R.
Sargent, Winthrop
Sprague, W. B.
Stanton, B. L.
Swayne, Wager
Tenney, Thomas
Thomas, E. B.
Waite, Morrison R.
Walker, Archibald B.
Walker, E. L.
Walton, Charles S.
Wilson, Noah

CHAPTER 24

WILLIAM P. CUTLER

THE OHIO LEGISLATURE AND

THE SECOND CONSTITUTIONAL CONVENTION

William P. Cutler, a member of the Whig Party, was first nominated for a seat in the House of Representatives of the Ohio Legislature in 1842, but was defeated at the election. In 1844, he was
again nominated and this time was successful in the election. Before
the close of the session, he had become the floor leader for his party.
In 1845 and 1846, he was re-elected and in the latter session, was

chosen as the Speaker of the House. In 1849, he was elected to represent Washington County at the Convention for a new Constitution of the State of Ohio.

The letters and documents that he wrote and received are part of the Letters and Documents of the Cutler Family in the Dawes Memorial Library of Marietta College. The list of the names of his correspondents follows:

Allen, Diarca Howe
Archbold, Edward
Ashland County, Ohio
Atwater, Caleb
Barker, George W.
Barker, Joseph, Jr.
Battelle, A.
Battelle, Ebenezer
Baxter, James
Bebb, Gov. William
Belpre & Cincinnati Railroad
Bennett, John Cook
Bosworth, D. P.
Bosworth, John W.
Bowen, James
Bradshaw, Thomas
Brown, D. W.
Browning, George
Buell, P. B.
Bureau, C. L. V.
Carpenter, S.
Carson, William
Chamberlain, John D.
Chandler, D.
Chapin, Harlow
Chares, John P.
Charles, John P.
Clarke, Melvin
Cooke, S. S.
Coolville, Ohio
Corner, Edwin
Cotton, John
Cowen, S.
Crawford, Robert
Creed, John M.
Cutler, Daniel
Cutler, Ephraim
Cutler, William

Davis, Marvil
Devol, Francis
Dodge, John
Dodge, J. S.
Durbin, James
Earl, William C.
Eaton, J. B.
Ellenwood, John
Ellis, Edward
Emerson, Caleb
Emrick, Joseph
Ennis, John B.
Ewart, Thomas W.
Ford, L. C.
Franklin & Washington Railroad
Gardner, Darwin E.
Gates, Beman
Gitteau, J. M.
Glover, Crawford
Goddard, Charles S.
Goodhue, N. W.
Greiner, John
Grimes, Alex
Halsey, D. W.
Hildreth, Samuel P.
Hitchcock, Reuben
Hocking City, Ohio
Holden, Joseph
Hollister, John J.
Janney, John J.
Jarvis, Dwight
Johns, Davis
Johnson, F. S.
Johnston, William
Kiddoo, John
King, J. W.
Laflin, Lyman
Lawson, Henry

CHAPTER 25

WILLIAM P. CUTLER AND

THE MARIETTA & CINCINNATI RAILROAD

William P. Cutler, in 1845, began a career that was to engage his attention for forty years, that of railroad construction and operation. This career began while he was a member of the Ohio House of Representatives when he was influential in securing a charter for a newly organized railroad company known as the Belpre & Cincinnati Railroad Company. In 1847 he was elected to a directorship of the company and in 1850, elected to the presidency, with the changing of the name to the Marietta & Cincinnati Railroad Company. In 1859, he organized a Board of Directors for the building of a connecting railroad from a point on the Ohio River known as Moore's Junction, building a branch line from there to Belpre, to be known for the next few years as the Union Railroad.

Finally, in 1884, some years after the Baltimore and Ohio Railroad had acquired the Marietta & Cincinnati road and had abandoned some parts of the line, a railroad from Moore's Junction was projected westward to Amesville to be known as the Marietta Mineral Railroad, thus tapping an area in Washington and Athens counties that abounded in coal mines.

The letters and documents for this part of Cutler's career are to be found in the Cutler Collections in the Dawes Memorial Library of Marietta College.

The following is the list of names of his correspondents for the above mentioned railroad companies:

American Immigrant Company
Andrews, Ebenezer B.
Austin, J.
Bachring, W. C.

Baldwin, C. P.
Baldwin, W. H.
Ballard, John
Baltimore & Ohio Railroad

Bartlett, S. W.
Battelle, Ebenezer
Beals, Jesse
Becker, M. J.
Beebe, Clinton
Belpre & Cincinnati Railroad
Bent, George E.
Binkley, H. S.
Briggs, C.
Brown, William A.
Bruce, Kneeland & Co.
Brummitt, John H.
Bundy, W. S.
Burney, Smith & Co.
Carville, K. L.
Chase, Miles & Co.
Cisler, J.
Civil War—Troop transportation
Clark, O. L.
Clarke, Helen M.
Collins, William O.
Conkling, Edgar
Cradle, Thomas
Crawford, William H.
Curtis, C. D.
Cutler, Ephraim
Cutler, William P.
Dale, Theodore E.
Dalton, John E.
Davis, Thomas B.
Dawes, Ephraim C.
Dennison, William
Diamond Iron Furnace
Dils, Pugsley & Co.
Dodge, F.
Drakeley & Co.
Dressen, W. C.
Durand, John
Eby, Seneca W.
Eichelberger, John M.
Ellis, L. N.
Ely, L. W.
Emerson, Caleb
Ferrie, James J.
Finch, Walter G.
Fish, H. C.
Frost, B. B.

Gabe, J. F.
Gale, L. M.
Garrett, John W.
Gates, Beman
Gist, E.
Glenn, William H.
Goodale & Co.
Greene, N. M.
Greenfield, Ohio
Grosvenor, Charles H.
Hagans & Broadwell
Halliday, Capt. W. P.
Hammedieu, L.
Harnden Express Company
Harsha, John M.
Hart, B. F.
Haseltine, Jacob
Hesseltine, Francis J.
Hillsborough & Cincinnati Railroad
Howes, J. H.
Hubbard, E. S.
Hutchins, John
Hyer, Jacob
Jarvis, W. R.
John, William
Kennedy, A.
Keys, Samuel B.
Kilvert, Charles A.
Kimball, C. P.
Kingsbury, Addison
Kingsbury, B. P.
Kip, Isaac
Latrobe, Benjamin
Leefe, George
Linscott, Frank
Littleboy, W. J.
Lord, I.
Low, Charles P.
Lyman, C. C.
McAboy, William
McArthurstown, Ohio
McCellan, George B.
McClintick, W. T.
McKim, William
McCoy, J. C.
McCoy, M. S.
McDowell, W. C.

McMurdie, W. S.
Madeira, John
Mains, William
Makin, Charles
Marietta & Cincinnati Railroad
Marietta Leader
Marietta Mineral Railroad
Maxwell, Samuel
Miles & Co.
Moore, E. C.
Moore, H. C.
Moore, Thomas W.
Morgan's Raid
Mounts, T. W.
Mowery, A. L.
Norris, George W.
Northrup, Colonel
Northwestern Virginia Railroad
Nye, William S.
Parker, George S.
Parker, J. Wyatt
Parkersburg, Virginia
Peabody, W. W.
Phillips, Robert E.
Pickering, B. C.
Pitzer, S. L.
Plumly, B. S.
Poor, Henry N.
Powell, Thomas
Price, William H.
Putnam, Douglas
Putnam, William R.
Quode, R. W.
Randolph, J. A.
Renick, Felix
Rice, Sabinus
Roads, Josiah
Rodgers, Nelson W.
Roelofson, W. F.
Rogers, J. S.
Ross, William
Schaffner, S.
Schutte, Daniel A.
Scioto Valley Railroad
Scott's Landing, Ohio

Seward, William H.
Shawnee & Hocking Railroad
Slane, Jackson
Smart, Hugh
Smith, Benjamin H.
Smith, B. M.
Smith, G. E.
Smith, John
Smith, Orland
Smith & Van Drizer Co.
Smith, Todd & Co.
Spencer, E. A.
Stansbury, Henry
Star Furnace Co.
Steamboat Transportation
Stewart, D. B.
Stone, Francis
Stone, D. W.
Stone, S. W.
Sullivant, William S.
Taft, Alphonso
Taft & Perry
Thurman, Allen G.
Trimble, Allen
Tuttle, Joseph F.
Twombly, R. S.
Van Winkle, P. G.
Vincent, Earl
Vincent, Henry
Vincent, O. B.
Vinton, Samuel F.
Walker, A. B.
Walker, Ezra
Waters, A. B.
Watson, William E.
Welch, John
Wheeling, Virginia
Williams, John
Wilson, Noah L.
Winslow, Lanier & Co.
Woodbridge, A. J.
Woodrow, Robert
Wright, D. S.
Zaleski, Ohio

CHAPTER 26

WILLIAM P. CUTLER

CONGRESS AND THE WAR YEARS

William P. Cutler was elected to the 37th Congress of the United States in 1860 from the Southeastern Ohio District by a plurality of 733 votes. He had been influential as a member of the Whig Party from the period when he entered the Ohio Legislature and the Second Ohio Constitutional Convention through the decade of the 1850's when the Republican Party was organized. He took his seat in the House of Representatives on July 4, 1861 when the Congress was called into extra session for the important duties of waging the Civil War.

While in Congress, he retained his position as vice-president of the Marietta & Cincinnati Railroad along with his congressional duties, recommending individuals in his district for Federal appointments, such as postmasterships, army promotions, soldier furloughs, wounded soldiers, and prisoners of war. His voluminous correspondence through this period reveals his concern about the soldiers in the field and their families at home. He was also in charge of recommending young men for the Military and Naval Academies. He ran again for Congress in 1863, but was defeated.

He succeeded, during the month of July, 1863, when his district was sorely threatened by the Morgan Raiders, in placing his railroad employees at strategic points along the Marietta & Cincinnati Railroad in order that transportation would not be molested. In his collection of letters and documents, he sent and received 128 telegrams to the officials of the Railroad and the commanders of the Ohio Militia.

From the close of his term in Congress from 1863 to the close of the War, he was often called upon by Federal officials for his advice in appointments to the Federal service.

The Culter Collection of Letters and Documents is to be found in the Dawes Memorial Library of Marietta College. The following are the names of his correspondents through the War years.

Abbot, Charles T.
Abbott, Samuel C.
Adair, James A.
Adams, Turner
Allen, A. G.
Allen, James
Amlin, Samuel
Andrews, Ebenezer B.
Andrews, Israel W.
Applegate, D.
Askins, William
Baldwin, J. C.
Barber, David
Bartlett, Francis
Bateman, Penrod
Beach, J. D.
Beatty, John A.
Berry, Austin
Blair, J. G.
Bosworth, Sala
Boyd, Charles A.
Brooks, John
Brown, George
Brown, Henry C.
Buell & Brother
Bundy, H. S.
Burgess, Dyer
Buckingham, Catharinus P.
Bull Run, Battle of
Cameron, Simon
Carrol, John
Chambers, David
Chandler, Capt. Albert
Chase, Salmon P.
Cheever, George B.
Clarke, Melvin
Cockrell, Francis M.
Coggeshall, W. T.
Conley, Thomas S.
Constable, R. E.
Corning, Erastus
Cresap, Thomas B.
Cunningham, E. E.

Cutler, Julia P.
Cutler, William P.
Cutler, Mrs. William P.
  (Elizabeth Williamson Voris)
Daniel, Thomas A.
Davis, Jefferson
Devol, D.
Dawes, Ephraim C.
Dawes, Lucinda Catherine "Kate"
  (Mrs. Samuel A. McLean)
Dawes, Rufus R.
Day, Russell H.
Denny, W. H. P.
Dilley, James
Douglas, Stephen A.
Douglas, W. H.
Durand, John
Elliott, Elijah
Elliott, Roger K.
Ellis, R. R.
Ellison, James
Embree, F. D.
Eward, Thomas W.
Ewing, Thomas
Fay, Catherine A.
Ferry, Orris S.
Flint Mills
Foote, Sen. Samuel A.
Gates, Beman
Goddard, General
Grosvenor, Mrs. T. A.
Hall, Lyman
Hamilton, James A.
Harbaugh, S. G.
Harris, John H.
Harsha, John M.
Harvey, G. W.
Haskins, A. L.
Henderson, David
Herron, John
Hildebrand, Jesse
Hildreth, Samuel P.
Hill, A. N.

Hillerill, David H.
Hollister, J. J.
Hooper, John
Hopper, R. D.
Horton, V. B.
Hubbard, William A.
Hugg, John H.
Hughes, David H.
Hueley, William
James, Charles T.
Jarvis, Dwight
Jones, John W.
Jones, W. A.
Kaufman, S. H.
Kearney, H. N.
Kellogg, J. A.
Kellogg, J. S.
Kendrick, H. H.
Kingsbury, Addison
Kinkead, Capt. J. B.
Knowles, Samuel S.
Kurtz, William W.
Lacey, Eliza
Lamont, Charles A.
Larzeliere, J. R.
Lexington Library Company
Library of Congress
Lincoln, Abraham
Little, Jacob
Lyon, W. M.
McLaughlin, James M.
McLean, Mrs. Samuel A.
    (Lucinda Catherine "Kate" Dawes)
Marietta & Cincinnati Railroad
Mills, John
Montgomery, Joab J.
Moore, T. W.
Moorehead, Joseph
Morgan's Raid
Morse, Peter
Mumford, T. J.
Norris, G. W.
Northrop, F. Jennings
Nye, Caroline M. S.
Nye, William S.
Ohio River, Flood
Ohio State Bank
Ohio State Journal

Pacific Railroad
Palmer, Addison
Palmer, J. E.
Parkersburg Bridge Bill
Patterson, John
Paxton, Col. J. C.
Pierrot, Eugene
Pilcher, William F.
Pinkerton, D. C.
Pond, Col. R. T.
Potwin, C. W.
Preston, J. C.
Putnam, Douglas
Putnam, William R.
Raff, Henry L.
Rand, George C.
Reamy, Thaddeus A.
Rhode Island Riflemen
Richardson, Joel S.
Richardson, Joseph
Robinson, L. B.
Ruff, Albert
Saunders, Maj. D. W.
Shellabarger, Samuel
Shepard, Hiram
Sherman, John
Shipley, Thomas B.
Shipman, Samuel
Shotwell, Thomas
Sibley, Hiram L.
Slavery
Slocomb, William
Smith, Mrs. Caleb B.
Smith, Orland
Smith, W. P.
Soldiers' Relief Society
Speer, Alex
Staats, Benoni
Stanberry, Henry
Stansbery, E. N.
Stillwell, Silas
Stimson, Rodney M.
Sturtevant, Justin J.
Sumner, Charles
Taft, Alphonso
Thurston, D. P.
Tod, Gov. David
Tompkins, James L.

CHAPTER 27

WILLIAM P. CUTLER, AND OTHER

RAILROAD CONSTRUCTION PROJECTS

1860-1873

William P. Cutler, in the 1860's, launched into the most hazardous period of his career. As stated earlier, he was in the United States Congress from 1861 to 1863, and while there he continued his duties as vice-president of the Marietta & Cincinnati Railroad. The capitalization of the railroad was far from satisfactory. Competition with the Baltimore & Ohio Railroad was becoming greater. In order that the fortunes of the Marietta & Cincinnati Railroad might be stabilized, he sent one of his associates, Noah L. Wilson, to London and Paris for foreign capital, but without avail since the Civil War was in progress.

However, he envisioned the new frontiers in establishing railroads, both in Ohio and into the states of the west. He saw opportunities for the building of a network of railroads in Southeastern Ohio, Kentucky and West Virginia, as well as in Indiana and Illinois. One of his visions was the building of a railroad from Marietta to the north, thus creating a rail outlet to the Pennsylvania Railroad in central Ohio.

Cutler's letters of the period, numbering some 250, are a part of the Cutler Collection of Letters and Documents in the Dawes Memorial Library of Marietta College.

The list of the names of the correspondents are as follows:

Alexander, Hugh
Andrews, Israel W.
Athens, Ohio
Austin, H. F.
Bachring, S. W.
Bachring, W. C.
Baltimore & Ohio Railroad
Bastian, John
Bates, J. A.
Beecher, C. A.
Bennett, William J.
Berry, Cornelius
Big Sandy Railroad
Bond, William J.
Bosworth, Wells & Co.
Bowen, Henry C.
Brindley, H. S.
Brown, A. G.
Brown, H. T.
Bundy, H. S.
Cadiz, Uhrichsville & Freeport
    Railroad
Campbell & Dawes
Carbondale & Shawneetown,
    (Illinois) Railroad
Carothers, N. O.
Carpenter, O.
Chamberlain, L. W.
Chesapeake & Ohio Railroad
Cincinnati, Hamilton & Dayton
    Railroad
Coal lands
Cochran, T. J.
Cowen, B. S.
Covington Iron Mill
Crawford, W. H.
Cutler, Mrs. Elizabeth V.
Cutler, Joseph J.

Cutler, William P.
Dale, E. R.
Danford, James
Dawes, Ephraim C.
Dawes, Rufus R.
Deming, Rev. Thomas
Dennison, Gov. William
DePriest, J. C.
Dodge, F.
Duck Creek Railroad
Dunfee, Z. S.
Durand, John
Emerson, William D.
Evansville & Cincinnati Railroad
Ewing, Thomas
Farm Affairs
Fayette County, Iowa
Fish, H. C.
Fleming, Morris J.
Foggitt, John
Fordyce, W.
Fosdick, W. R.
Foss, Rodney
Frazier, W. H.
Frisbee, D. G.
Frost & Co.
Fullerton, William
Fulton, W. L.
Gallipolis & Pomeroy Railroad
Galloway, A. J.
Gates, Beman
George, Robert
Glazier, A. B.
Goodwin, J. A.
Goodwin, J. M.
Graham & Thomas
Green, Thomas
Green, W. A.

Greene, J. B.
Greene, W. A.
Grindstone Industry
Grow, George B.
Gurley, William H.
Gurney, N. A.
Guthrie, Edwin
Hall, B.
Hall, T. J.
Harmar, Ohio
Harsha, D. C.
Hartshorn, Isaac
Harvey, S. W.
Henderson, Captain
Hesseltine, Francis J.
Hibbard, J. R.
Hibbard, Rebecca
Hope Furnace
Hopkins, Mark
Hornaus, J. S.
Howland, Francis
Hunter, Morton C.
Hutchins, J.
Hyer, Jacob
Illinois Railroads
Illinois Southeastern Railroad
Illinois Southwestern Railroad
Iron Mountain,
    Chester & Eastern Railroad
Jackson, George W.
Jessup, W. H.
Jewett, Judge Thomas L.
Johnson, W. V.
Johnson, W. W.
Jones, Charles Floyd
Jones, Gen. W. S.
Kansas, State of, Lands
Keys, S. B.
Kilvert, S. W.
King, John, Jr.
Kingsbury, D. P.
Kunz, Mrs. John
Larkin, Stillman C.
Lawrence, J. J.
Leonard, W.
Lexington, (Ky.) & Big Sandy
    Railroad

Linscott, Frank
Livesay, G. W.
Livestock Industry
Lord, Abner
Lytle, James
McCabe, Robert
McClintick, W. T.
McClintick & Smith
McClure, W.
McConnelsville Oil Refinery
McIlvaine, Judge George W.
Madeira, John
Male, Adam
Male, James
Marietta & Cincinnati Railroad
Marietta & Pittsburgh Railroad
Marietta Iron Works
Marietta Rolling Mill
Mathews, J. B.
Maxwell, Rev. L. W.
Means, John
Mills, John
Missouri Lands
Moore, E. H.
Moore, T. W.
Morgan, Henry
Morris, Charles
Morton, Isaac
Mower, E. M.
Mower, Mrs. J. C.
Munn & Co.
Munsell, W.
Nash, Judge Simeon
New York Independent
Newton, Stephen
Noble, Rev. J.
Noble County, Ohio
Norris, George W.
Older, E. B.
O'Neal Trial
Oregon County, Missouri
Ormiston, John
Paint Creek Valley Railroad
Pana & Springfield Railroad
Paola & Fall River Railroad
Parker, E. W.
Patterson, John

Peabody, W. W.
Pearce, F. E.
Peck, A. P.
Pennsylvania Railroad
Perkins, C. A.
Perkins, William H.
Piatt, Donn
Pierce, Winslow S.
Pinkerton, D. C.
Pitzer, S. L.
Plants, T. J.
Plumly, E. L.
Poor, H. D.
Poor, H. W.
Portsmouth Railroad
Powell, J. F.
Presbyterian Church
Pruden, Isaiah
Putnam, David
Putnam, Douglas
Putnam, William Pitt
Putnam, William R.
Randolph, J. A.
Rice, H. J.
Richards, Joseph H.
Richardson, Mrs. Esther
Ridgway, Thomas S.
Riggs, Josiah
Rogers Locomotive Works
Roudebush, William
Salt Deposits
Schutte, D.
Sechler, D. M.
Seiss, Rev. J.
Shawneetown Rolling Mill
Sheep Raising
Sherman, John
Smith, Gen. Orland
Smith, Samuel B.

Smith & Morris
Society for Theological and
    Collegiate Education
Southern Illinois Railroad
Southwestern Ohio Railroad
Spencer, J. C.
Stafford, Martin
Stansbury, E. M.
Starnes, A.
Stearns, W. L.
Still, Thomas
Stimson, Rodney M.
Stone, Loring E.
Stone, S. W.
Temperance Movement
Thompson, J. Edgar
Turner, W. S.
Tuttle, Joseph F.
Vinton County, Ohio
Vinton Iron Furnace
Wade, Benjamin F.
Walker, Archibald B.
Wallin, Rev. J. G.
Ward, Langdon S.
Warner, A. J.
Washington County Military History
Waters, A. B.
Waters, I. R.
Webb, William
Wells, George H.
Wescott, J. W.
Wilcox, John
Wilcox, L. A.
Wilcox, Thomas B.
Wilson, Thomas B.
Winslow, Gen. E. S.
Wool Industry
Wright, George C.

CHAPTER 28

WILLIAM P. CUTLER AND

THE CLOSING YEARS OF HIS LIFE

William P. Cutler, who had, in his active life, become well known for his public services as a legislator, a leader in Presbyterian Church circles, and an industrialist in railroad building, sought semi-retirement in the years following 1873 when he moved to Marietta.

The grandson of the Rev. Manasseh Cutler, one of the principal leaders in the settlement of Ohio and the son of Ephraim Cutler, one of the early settlers, turned his attention to gathering historical data of the founding of Ohio for the Centennials which would be celebrated in 1876 of the Declaration of Independence and 1888 of the founding of the first settlement of the Northwest Territory at Marietta.

In his closing years he contributed historical articles to national magazines, and with the help of his sister, Julia Perkins Cutler, prepared the copy for the biographies of his grandfather and father. He was one of the leaders in the founding of the Ohio Archaeological and Historical Society. His last public service was that of general chairman of the Marietta Centennial celebration of 1888. His death occurred on April 11, 1889.

The Cutler Collection of Letters and Documents includes his articles and letters, covering the final phase of his life, which are to be found in the Dawes Memorial Library of Marietta College.

The names of his principal correspondents and the subjects are as follows.

Account books, 1867-1889
Adams, John Quincy
Allison, Nancy
Amestown, Church of
Andrews, Ebenezer B.
Andrews, Israel Ward

Athens County, History
Athens Messenger
Atwater, Lyman H.
Bailey, Mrs. E. S.
Ballard, Julia Barker
Barker, Joseph

CHAPTER 29

JULIA PERKINS CUTLER

Julia Perkins Cutler, the second daughter of Ephraim and Sally (Parker) Cutler, was born at the OLD STONE HOUSE in Warren Township, Washington County on January 24, 1814 and died, unmarried, in Marietta, December 18, 1904. The middle name, Perkins was acquired from an early ancestor of the Dawes-Cutler Family line, named John Perkins, 1614-1686, of New England.

Julia, throughout her life-span of 90 years occupied an important position in the family as a homemaker, scribe and historian. Along with the practical duties of managing a home for her father and mother, her brother William Parker Cutler, his wife who was often in critical health and their children, five of whom died in their infancy, she found time for her writings of the early annals of the settlement, the genealogical data of the family and her correspondence with her family relatives, without which much would have been lost from the collection of Cutler Letters and Documents.

She was educated, first in private schools, and later in the Granville Female Seminary. In a letter dated May 28, 1835, she wrote that she was teaching a school of 34 pupils. She frequently wrote poems, gathering her subjects from the scenic vistas from her home window, the Ohio River and the surrounding hills.

The following is a list of her principal historical productions, now housed in the Dawes Memorial Library:

1. The ancestral lines of the Cutler Family.

2. A summary of Ephraim Cutler's experiences in the Ohio Legislature, 1819-1825.

3. Scrapbooks, compiled from newspapers, 1839-1904.

4. Handwritten copies of the Reminiscences of Joseph Barker.

5. Warren Township Recollections.

6. Military Records of the soldiers from Warren Township in the Civil War.

7. Recollections of the founders of Amestown, besides the Cutlers, the Browns and the family of Lt. George Ewing.

8. Diaries, 1838, 1848, 1849-1850, 1854, 1858, and the day by day accounts of the Civil War from April, 1861 to 1864.

9. Diary, July 1863, "Our experience during Morgan's Raid."

10. Correspondence from and to her nieces and nephews of the Dawes family, Rufus R. Dawes and his brother, Ephraim C. Dawes, both of whom were officers during the Civil War, Henry Manasseh Dawes, and nieces, Lucinda Catherine Dawes, (Kate), and Lucy and Sarah Jane Dawes, the latter, the wife of Rev. John Haskell Shedd, both missionaries in Persia.

11. The Life, Journals and Correspondence of her grandfather, Manasseh Cutler, published in 1888.

12. The Life and Times of her father, Ephraim Cutler.

13. The Founders of Ohio, Brief sketches of the Forty-Eight Pioneers.

14. Letters from and to her sister, Clarissa, the wife of Rev. James H. Walton, her half sister, Mary, Mrs. Gulliver Dean, and her brother, Daniel Converse Cutler.

15. Poem, "The Old Homestead."

CHAPTER 30

SARAH JANE CUTLER

Sarah Jane Cutler, the daughter of William P. and Elizabeth (Voris) Cutler, was born at THE OLD STONE HOUSE in Warren Township in 1856. She was the only child of the six brothers and sisters in the family to survive beyond childhood. In 1872-1873, she moved with the members of her family to Marietta where she lived until her death in 1933.

She, after the death of her aunt, Julia Perkins Cutler, 1904, carried on the family tradition of preserving the letters and documents of the Cutler family. In her own right, she was the author of pioneer stories and historical articles, including a history of the Warren Presbyterian Church, and later, that of the First Presbyterian Church of Marietta. Being of the missionary spirit she also followed the fortunes of the family of her cousin Sarah Jane Dawes, the wife of the Rev. John Haskell Shedd and her family who were missionaries in Persia for thirty-one years.

The following is a selected list of her writings which are now a part of the Cutler Collection of Letters and Documents in the Dawes Memorial Library of Marietta College:

Notes on the old buildings in Marietta, Newport and Belpre.
Chicago, diary, 1871
History of the Warren Presbyterian Church.
A catalog of the Warren Church Library.
English gardens and rural scenes
The story of Jacob David of Urumia
The elevated square in Marietta
Critique, The Enjoyment of Poetry
Niagara Falls in 1861.

GENERAL INDEX

The Letters and Documents of the Cutler Collection are alphabetically listed by the names of the correspondents and their subjects in the preceding Table of Contents of chapters numbering from 1 to 30, and designated as follows: by the arabic numbers:

Cutler, Ephraim—1, 2, 3, 4, 5, 6, 7, 8, 9, 10, 11, 12, 13, 14, 15, 16, 17, 18, 19, 20, 24, 25.

Cutler, Jervis ——1, 3, 4, 5, 6, 16, 18.

page one hundred

ルタ5

ル- 1 ワ5

A ワ ワ 5